Walking, Writing and Performance
Autobiographical Texts by Deirdre Heddon, Carl Lavery and Phil Smith

This book is dedicated to:

- my Dad, and his new knees (DH)
- my Mum and Brother, Ann and Gareth Lavery (CL)
- the memory of my zayde, Samuel Mock, who made at least one extraordinary walk that I can barely imagine (RM)
- my late Nan and Pop for inspiring *The Crab Walks*, to my Mum and Dad for inspiring *Crab Steps Aside*, and to my daughter, Rachel, for inspiring my continuing 'splorin' (PS)

Walking, Writing and Performance
Autobiographical Texts by Deirdre Heddon, Carl Lavery and Phil Smith

Edited by
Roberta Mock

intellect Bristol, UK / Chicago, USA

First published in the UK in 2009 by
Intellect Books, The Mill, Parnall Road, Fishponds, Bristol, BS16 3JG, UK

First published in the USA in 2009 by
Intellect Books, The University of Chicago Press, 1427 E. 60th Street, Chicago,
IL 60637, USA

A catalogue record for this book is available from the British Library.

Cover designer: Holly Rose
Copy-editor: Rebecca Vaughan-Williams
Typesetting: Mac Style, Beverley, E. Yorkshire

ISBN 978-1-84150-155-0

Printed and bound by Gutenberg Press, Malta.

CONTENTS

Introduction: It's (Not Really) All About Me, Me, Me

Roberta Mock

In my view walking slows everything down, almost as if one's legs were braking the very revolution of the earth itself. It is, quite frankly, the only possible response to a civilisation crazed with its own sense of mobility; for, by walking to one's appointments, you introduce the relative timelessness of physical geography into the transitory deliberations of the human psyche.

(Will Self)[1]

MAKE A WALK WRITE A TEXT READ IT TO AN AUDIENCE. BODY AND VOICE.
(Hamish Fulton)[2]

This book originated from a rather basic observation. While attending the 'Site/Sight' symposium at Exeter University in September 2004,[3] it occurred to me that (at least) three people whom I knew fairly well generated autobiographical performance texts by engaging with the fluid relationships between specific places. I simply noticed that, for Dee Heddon, Carl Lavery and Phil Smith – all in very different ways – the acts of walking, remembering and writing, and thus the construction of narrative self and performance spaces, were intimately related.

Otherwise, and certainly on the surface of things, I am not the most obvious person to guide you into a book about performance practices related to walking. Nobody would describe me as a walker by inclination, experience, or temperament. I ascribe this to the fact that I am from the Motor City ... I'm afraid that's not quite true. Perhaps even more significantly, I'm from somewhere just outside metropolitan Detroit where it is even more imperative that one is able to drive.[4] There were, for example, few pavements (or sidewalks, as we called them) on my just-under-a-mile walk to school, undertaken during one of the few life stages when one wasn't expected to move everywhere by car (not to mention in a historical moment when children were still expected to walk to school).

I am from 'the suburbs' and, if there's one thing that's rather noticeable in autobiographical accounts of walking, it's that walking tends to occur in either rural or urban environments rather than in the hinterlands between the two. There may be a reason for this, art-historically speaking, beyond the dearth of permissible routes through a landscape of clearly demarcated privately owned plots. In 1967, the year that Francesco Careri identifies as 'the year of walking'[5] – while I was tucked up in my suburban cot under a sequence of wooden Disney characters – the American artist Robert Smithson wrote an article for *Artforum* entitled 'The Monuments of Passaic' and presented a related exhibition of his work at a New York gallery. For *The Tour of the Monuments of Passaic, New Jersey*, Smithson set off on a 'suburban odyssey' of the city in which he was born and then mounted the photographic traces of this journey. The images of Passaic's empty streets, blunt metal pipes, disorientating bridges and obsolete machinery that he chose to share in this exhibition add up to a vision of a suburbia that Smithson evidently considered shallow, mimetic, false, and always already incomplete:

> the suburbs exist without a rational past and without the 'big events' of history. Oh, maybe there are a few statues, a legend, and a couple of curios, but no past, just what passes for a future. A Utopia minus a bottom [...]. Passaic seems full of 'holes' compared to New York City, which seems tightly packed and solid, and those holes in a sense are the monumental vacancies that define, without trying, the memory-traces of an abandoned set of futures. Such futures are found in grade B Utopian films, and then imitated by the suburbanite.[6]

In a cultural landscape that valued conceptual originality, Smithson had both been there and done that for those interested in the creative potentials of suburban walking. Furthermore, at one of the (admittedly many) moments that heralded the birth of aesthetic walking practice, the suburbs were deemed and represented as void and empty, denied a legitimate sense of past or future and, perhaps even worse, of either the present or (human) presence.

The bonding of thickly laid temporal dimensions through embodiment is absolutely fundamental to the creative practices you will read (and read about) in this book. *The Crab Walks* and *Crab Steps Aside* are performance texts made by Phil Smith based on his exploratory walking of an area of South Devon where he was taken for childhood holidays and then, later on, in Munich, Herm and San Gimignano. *Mourning Walk* is a performance that developed from a walk Carl Lavery made to mark the anniversary of his father's death. In *Tree*, the result of a multi-disciplinary collaborative process, Dee Heddon occupies a single square foot of a garden in Exeter, making vivid spatial and temporal connections through an 'extroverted' autobiographical practice that links personal, cultural and collective memories. It is perhaps not surprising that Andreas Huyssen describes the attraction of memory as 'an attempt to

Phil Smith in his 'map' shirt, performing *Crab Steps Aside* (2005). Photo: Derek Frood

slow down the pace of life, to resist the dissolution of time and space in the synchronicity of the electronic archive, to recover a mode of contemplation outside the universe of simulation and fast speed information'.[7] Huyssen could equally be describing the appeal of walking (compare this passage to Will Self's psychogeographic epigraph at the start of this Introduction).

The temporal and spatial nature of the walking differs substantially in each case in this book. Carl plotted an eighteen-mile course with the help of his mother, from Market Harborough in Leicestershire to Cottesmore in Lincolnshire, and walked it in a single day. Phil's various walks took place over an extended period of time in a variety of locations, stopping and starting, resisting predetermined routes by scuttling sideways and following his instincts by moving 'like a crab'. Dee's use of walking makes explicit the complex networks between histories, storytelling, imagination, site, and autobiography that connect all three artists. As she discusses in her essay, by repeatedly walking within a small area beneath a Sequoia tree and by acknowledging that to stand still at the same site 'is to have arrived', she finds herself able to imaginatively travel across continents and centuries and to walk empathically in those places. Time, space and body fold together through kinaesthesia.

As Carl asks in his *Mourning Walk*, echoing the writer W.G. Sebald: '[M]ight it not be that we also have an appointment to keep in the past, in what has gone before and is for the most part extinguished, and must go there in search of places and people who have some connection with us on the far side of time, so to speak?' Later, in the essay that accompanies his autobiographical script, Carl notes that the further he advanced in real time and space, the more he seemed to lose himself in memory and daydream. He writes that: 'There were times, for instance, on the walk, when I had the impression that past and present had entirely collapsed, and that I had magically returned to other landscapes which, for some reason or other, had, until that moment, remained hidden and out of reach.'

Similarly, in *The Crab Walks*, Phil Smith explains that via the act of walking, he 'wanted to travel not just back and forward across time, but also across a little of the sensibility of this planet'. By looking for his own story, he finds other stories: 'this walk through nostalgia is a walk into the future, a pioneering wander through the familiar, only to find everything changed and full of endless wonder. But the wonder looks back at you, looks into you, and you look back at it'. Phil's use of the word 'nostalgia' here is rather brave since, for some commentators, nostalgia refers to a sentimental, regressive and reactionary response to the present by evoking the desire for a past that never was. For others, like Phil, it opens up the potential for a range of historically informed critical dialogues. In either case, nostalgia is politically charged and implicated. As Mieke Bal has observed, 'nostalgic discourse can take on all the different values any discursive mode can take on, depending on context and use'.[8] This is well illustrated by Dee Heddon's analysis of *The Crab Walks* in which she writes that, while it is tempting to read Phil's performance text

> as driven by a nostalgic longing for a rosy past where, with the benefit of hindsight, the self was known to be safe and secure (and loved) ... Smith's walking and storying work

together against this pull [...]. This is not, then, in any way a nostalgic return to some past place. The places and times that Smith conjures are always multiple, reflecting his layered sense of 'self'.[9]

There are, in fact, several critical models available to discuss productive, complex heterogeneous nostalgic practices; Dee, for instance, applies Jennifer Ladino's term 'counter-nostalgia' which envisions a return to a 'home' that is layered, fragmented and complicated.

We might, however, choose to employ Svetlana Boym's distinctions between reflective and restorative nostalgias when considering the type of performance work presented in this volume. In her analysis of post-communist urban cultures, Boym observes that, 'If restorative nostalgia ends up reconstructing emblems and rituals of home and homeland in an attempt to conquer and spatialize time, reflective nostalgia cherishes shattered fragments of memory and temporalizes space'.[10] While restorative nostalgia is intended to shore up nationalist imaginings of a mythic collective past and future, reflective nostalgia positions the individual in a flexible historical trajectory. As Carl tells us in *Mourning Walk*, 'When I walk, I go back and forth in an infinite journey between memory and imagination.' Reflective nostalgia is about movement and homelessness as much as it is about the impossible destination called 'home'. Its operation and production seem to echo Dee's application of the term 'autotopography' to describe a practice that 'brings into view the "self" that plots place and that plots self in place, admitting (and indeed actively embracing) the subjectivity and inevitable partiality or bias of that process'.[11]

And so, please indulge me while I return us to Robert Smithson's representations of Passaic, New Jersey, made some 40 years ago. Smithson's suburbs resist nostalgic impulses of any kind and are strangely removed from any sense of self (except a dying one). They are not 'familiar' like the landscapes conjured by Phil Smith. They neither hold nor reveal stories; they do not hide other landscapes, like Carl Lavery's, within themselves. According to Careri, 'There is no enjoyment, no satisfaction, no emotional involvement in walking through the nature of suburbia.' Smithson's suburbs are metaphors for 'the periphery of the mind, the rejects of thought and culture',[12] and while such peripheries and their architectural ruins hold an interest for Phil Smith as well, Smithson's suburban imagery stands for forgetting, for forging a new nature via disintegration rather than the hybridization of collective memory. The 'suburbanites' of Smithson's Passaic are referred to, but conspicuously and negligently absent, trapped inside insubstantial little houses on the outskirts of industrial zones which are themselves peripheral to the wholeness of the city.

This, however, wasn't *my* experience of suburbia. For me, the suburb was indeed in a state of constant transformation but not because it was returning to some structural wilderness. It was young, thrusting and overburdened with the ephemerality of the 'now'; it may indeed have existed outside the histories of grand narratives but it was hardly free from representation as Smithson implied. Rather, my suburb – or perhaps the suburb of my memory – is what Phil Smith might call a 'dread space', a location which expresses the uncanny 'dynamic between a displaced localness and the desire for nowhere'.[13] And while it may have constantly struggled with a sense of displacement, it did so in its own peculiarly local manner while negotiating its role in the very concept of what a city means.

Nevertheless, by the time I might have been able to embrace walking as an act of definition and creative freedom, *my* suburb of Detroit was not a place one would naturally think to walk a 'mixture of stories and stones' (as Phil describes his journey in *Crab Walks*). Nor, far from the cosmopolitan art markets, was one likely to have encountered the idea of aesthetic walking; it could even be argued that, if you *had* (for example, by reading Smithson in an old issue of *Artforum*) and were attracted to the idea, you were more likely to leave the suburbs in search of those like-minded individuals. In any case, in those days before experiencing David Lynch's *Blue Velvet*, my immediate landscape didn't seem to call out for close exploration and certainly not by foot; by the time I *had* seen this movie, I had also moved on, to places that seemed less dreadful and with better public transport systems.[14]

You may be wondering why I'm telling you all this. I'm sure that the primary contributors to this volume would agree that where one starts is crucial to the mapping of a journey, not to mention to its outcome. And the fact that *I* have made such a journey (perhaps especially from such inauspicious beginnings) is crucial to understanding the work you are about to read by Phil, Carl and Dee. You neither have to be a rambler, a *flaneur*, or a situationist, nor want to know about the lives of these three individuals to engage with this book. Yes, of course, their writings are autobiographical, but they hinge around the production of self-revelation that is ours, rather than solely or primarily theirs. As Phil writes in his contextual essay:

> In *The Crab Walks* and *Crab Steps Aside*, I set out to place the autobiographical in an instrumental role [...]. In both pieces I often say that I cannot remember things, that strong emotional memories evaporate in the face of their supposed sites, that what I felt most strongly mine came to feel alien and shared [...]. But it was not the silencing of the autobiographical that I was after: rather the mythologizing of it. And not my own in particular, but anyone's. To bring the autobiographical into a play of generalities.

Central to this operation is the recognition of agency and of performativity.

The texts you are about to read, whether they appear to be play scripts or critical or reflexive essays, are all examples of what Peggy Phelan has called performative writing. In *Mourning Sex*, she explains it in these terms:

> Performative writing is an attempt to find a form for 'what philosophy wishes all the same to say.' Rather than describing the performance event 'in direct signification,' a task I believe to be impossible and not terrifically interesting, I want this writing to enact the affective force of the performance event again.[15]

The documentations of and/or blueprints for performances in this book are themselves attempting to find a form through which to distil the experiences of previous performance events: that is, those that Carl describes here as 'pedestrian performances'. The languages used to do this have been directly generated by the performances themselves. They present rather than represent; they evoke subjectivity rather than attempting to describe an experience objectively. It is important that each of the autobiographical playtexts refers to the processes of its own genesis, composition and construction.

The affective force being enacted through these languages is one that aims to propel the reader into taking responsibility for making her own performative gestures. Phil, Dee and Carl are doing things with words; on the evidence of their texts, I believe they would now be very happy if, having experienced their work, you did something (however small or large) with or in your life. This is, perhaps, another of Robert Smithson's legacies. As Careri notes, the invitation to the audience of Smithson's Passaic exhibition and readers of his *Artforum* article was clear: they should 'go with the artist/revealer/guide along the Passaic River to explore a "land that time forgot"'.[16] Although Smithson advocated the renting of a car to do so, he was *almost* certainly referring to the accessibility of Passaic and not the mode of exploration once there. There is, however, an ambiguous sense that Smithson might have been suggesting that it was possible to view the decontextualized significant moments of *his* journey through car windows (as one might track a gamekeeper in an exoticized safari game park), rather than discovering one's own resonating monuments by foot as he did.

This possibility is one of several significant distinctions to be made between Smithson's prototypical work and that of the writers in this book. Another is that the places represented by Phil, Carl and Dee are nearly always figured as cumulative rather than entropic. These places are smothered with life histories. While Smithson's 1967 work seemed to bleakly celebrate a postindustrial landscape that could be viewed abstractly as formally monumental, what our autobiographical writers seek for themselves and others tends to be human in scale and personally meaningful. At the end of his performances, Phil distributes maps and other ephemera (that he has usually created with designer Tony Weaver) to encourage walking, exploration and reflection by audience members. On the back of the folder of cards I received at the end of *Crab Steps Aside*, the 'instructions for use' read as follows:

Put in a safe place and forget
Enjoy them for themselves
Use as triggers for your own walks
Tear up and throw away
An 'album' to make new maps for
Make into place mats
To re-explore
Something else

Similarly, at the end of *Tree*, Dee sings, 'You can find or make a route, my story in your story'.

As Laura Marcus has noted in her book *Auto/biographical Discourses*, the concept of performativity is a common denominator for a wide variety of autobiographical and life writing practices. She observes that even though the performative is defined in some quite radically different ways, it can be used to indicate shared tendencies (all of which resonate in this project as well):

> the valorisation of personal histories, a stress on the positional, a certain anti-theoreticism, a sense of importance of 'speaking out' as a way of authorising identity while at the same time identity is said to be performatively constituted rather than pre-discursive.[17]

If such tendencies are notable in discussions about contemporary auto/biographical writing, they are equally evident in two other discourses that intersect with them in this book: that is, those of performance and of landscape. All rely on the masquerade of authenticity to suggest contingency and the embodiment of stories is often central to this.

Doreen Massey, a geographer whose ideas have been enthusiastically embraced by many performance researchers, offers a conception of space that is interrelational, multiple and always under construction. In her book, *For Space*, she describes it as 'the dimension of multiple trajectories, a simultaneity of stories-so-far'.[18] According to Mike Pearson, a performance maker and theorist who has certainly influenced – if not perhaps directly inspired – much of the material in this book, 'Just as landscapes are constructed out of the imbricated actions and experiences of people, so people are constructed in and dispersed through their habituated landscape: each individual, significantly, has a particular set of possibilities in presenting an account of their own landscape: *stories*.'[19] He describes the written text of *In Comes I*, his most recent reflection on landscape, memory and autobiographical performance, as performative multivalent story-telling in which the context and action of analysis are interdependent.

There is certainly a danger of blurring the acts of writing and performance via the promiscuity of the performative. For instance, my response to Phil's, Dee's and Carl's performance texts and commentaries is the 'personal criticism' you are reading now (a form that, as Phelan notes, is a kissing cousin of both the autobiographical essay and performative writing). This, according to Nancy Miller, entails the staging of my own relationship to the ideas I am encountering as a critic. 'By turning its authorial voice into spectacle,' she writes, 'personal writing theorizes its own performance: a personal materialism'.[20] I would perhaps go even further to describe personal writing as an embodied practice that performs its own theory. It is important to remember, however, that if I am indeed now performing, you are not present at the moment this performance is taking place. While I am displaying the construction of my becoming to you and for you, there is no dialogic process between us.[21]

Indeed, as Dee Heddon has noted elsewhere, such processes of exchange between performers and spectators can be considered one of the most productive aspects of the relationship between performance's materiality (which, I should note, is not to be confused with Nancy Miller's 'personal materialism') and performative agency: many performers who activate the power of the autobiographical mode 'simultaneously place the referent into a situation of instability, prompting us to question the status of what we see'. Dee maintains 'that the challenge for all autobiographical performance is to harness the dialogic potential afforded by the medium, using it in the service of difference rather than sameness'.[22] Such critical autobiographical practices intersect in important ways with the radical research practices and interventions that have been advocated by performance scholars such as Dwight Conquergood. Conquergood evoked Michel de Certeau's aphorism, 'what the map cuts up, the story cuts across', to explain how radical performance research should take account of 'local contexts' and transnational narratives while travelling between two types of knowledge: official abstract 'maps' and personal embodied 'stories'. In doing so, he drew attention not just to the importance of the *movement between* different locations and histories, but also to debates about the relative values of and within binaries such as performance/text:

> We challenge the hegemony of the text best by reconfiguring texts and performances in horizontal, metonymic tension, not by replacing one hierarchy with another, 'the romance of performance for the authority of the text.[23]

The affective value of the work in this volume rests precisely in the ways in which this challenge has been embraced by its authors.

Dee, Carl and Phil seem to tell us very little about the processes of writing itself. Given the openness with which they discuss their lives and have meticulously mapped the interrelationships of other creative processes, I have come to believe that all three must feel that they *did* implicitly write about them. As such, I propose that their writing processes are probably more closely akin to devising and dramaturgical practices than those of the 'solitary' writer or dramatist. This is writing for and as performance and, following on, their writing practices probably emphasize decision-making, editing and shaping over imagining and speculating. The latter two actions will have taken place during the walk itself and on subsequent reflections about it, rather than during the construction of the playtext itself. There are, however, similar processes at work in the acts of walking and choosing appropriate language with which to communicate experience. According to the philosopher Brian Massumi,

> When we walk, we're dealing with the constraint of gravity. There's also the constraint for balance and the need for equilibrium. But, at the same time, to walk you need to throw off the equilibrium, you have to let yourself go into a fall, then you cut it off and regain the balance [...].

> It's similar with language. I see it as a play between constraint and room to manoeuvre...

> The common paradigm approaches experience as if we were somehow outside it, looking in, like disembodied subjects handling an object. But our experiences aren't objects. They're us. They're what we're made of. We *are* our situations, we *are* our moving through them. We *are* our participation.[24]

In articulating the ideas that are conjured through movement, Phil, Carl and Dee mimic both the opportunities and limitations of walking itself. This critical and imaginative use of convention results in the production of affect, which Massumi also relates to feelings of 'hope'. Affect, for him, refers to 'where we might be able to go and what we might be able to do' in every present situation.[25]

There are many ways to engage with published performance texts and one of the most common is to actually perform them. Although it is usually assumed that published play scripts can (and should) be staged, directed and acted by other people in other spaces at some point in the future, the most likely initial response to the writing for performance presented and discussed in this volume is that it is meant to be embodied by those who first created it. There are, however, certainly other more graphic and visual ways of presenting the written intersection of walking, performance and autobiography (although even these forms of presentation do not necessarily preclude new interpretations by other performers).[26] Although (or, perhaps, because) Phil, Dee and Carl each (re)staged their exchanges with specific sites in more conventionally 'theatrical' contexts, our decision to present their performances in this seemingly conventional textual manner raises complex issues that relate to the purpose of publishing autobiographical scripts.

What happens when you perform somebody else's autobiographical performance text? Is it still autobiographical? How precisely does its meaning change? Is there fundamentally any difference between the 'autobiographical actor' and any other? As Shirley Neuman has noted, 'Theorists of autobiography...have outlined various poetics that attempt to explain how the narrator of autobiography, indexed as an "I," creates a "self" in the text and establishes, or cannot establish, a referential relation between that "self" and a "self"-in-the-world that may, or may not, exist apart from its discursive production'.[27] How do these poetic explanations mutate and slip when the 'I' and the 'self' move beyond text via more than one performative operation?

In an attempt to explore some of these questions – indeed, to even discover whether they are valuable and appropriate questions to pose – I decided to perform one of the scripts in this book myself.[28] I chose Dee's *Tree: A Studio Performance*. I would like to make it clear that this had nothing to do with the fact that we're both women and of generally similar ages; I was not interested in either passing as Dee or in being believable. Quite the contrary. When I asked Dorinda Hulton (who led the collaborative devising process described by Dee in her essay) for her permission to perform the text, I struggled to find a word for what I wanted to do with it. She suggested that I was going to 'act' and, for some reason, this made me deeply uncomfortable. But it was a very apt word, for 'to act' doesn't simply refer to mimetic representation; it also means to operate, to be, to do.

I am not a particularly 'good' – that is, convincing – actor in the conventional sense; I am a fairly charismatic performer, though, and this usually has something to do with my hair.[29] By 'not good', I also mean 'not very skilled at remembering lines'. In conceiving the project, there were very few guiding principles, but one was that I had to perform all the words that the author had intended to say in his or her performance. This meant that I needed to choose the shortest of the three texts here. I also decided to perform to camera, originally anticipating that the process (and its aesthetic result) would resemble the documentation of a sited live performance event.[30] And so, I must remind you that I am not a walker by inclination, experience, or temperament. Dee's script had many advantages: I didn't have to walk far or for days and her tree was within a couple miles of my house.

My main strategy was to return the performing body to the site of the text in order to provoke a discussion about the instabilities of autobiographical narratives, the relationships between intertextualities and embodiment, and the 'authenticity' of located memory as coherent story. The primary reason for this was to by-pass assumptions that accrue in 'traditional' theatre (which overlaps with, but is not identical to, theatre in traditional spaces): that is, the tendency to accept the separation of authorial voice from the voice produced by a specific performing body, as well as narrative time and place from the here and now of performance. I do not wish to imply that this is necessarily a bad thing. As Dan Rebellato has provocatively argued, a 'play in performance' by a writer like Sarah Kane or Martin Crimp is inherently 'site-unspecific' due to 'its non-identical quality, its ability to be both general and particular, its ability to express and articulate a kind of theatrical cosmopolitanism'. It is this, he argues, that produces the ethical value that distinguishes them from both 'McTheatre' (such as globalized, factory-produced productions of big musicals) or the site-specificity of artists like Richard Serra (who famously argued that his public artwork, *Tilted Arc*, could not be resited without destroying the politically resistant value that resided in its local specificity).[31] I took yet another approach, aiming to achieve the creation of temporal and spatial dissonance in which more than one particular locality and more than one particular body and more than one particular voice shimmered, problematically, in and out of view.

Like Dee's, my process of creating and staging what was eventually simply called *Tree* was a collaborative one; unlike her version – and partly to mediate against and destabilize assumptions of the camera's authoritative status – my collaborator intervened into the very fabric of the performance text.[32] *Tree* was made with Siobhan Mckeown, who is a film-maker with substantial experience of live performance documentation; she is, not coincidentally, also my daughter. Siobhan's 'voice' is presented in subtitles that were originally intended to undermine the authenticity of the words I speak. For instance, when I claim that 'my dad was a forester', Siobhan's voice – in writing at the bottom of the screen – says 'my grandfather was a banker'. The 'fact' that I am not, and cannot be, Dee is reinforced by the Siobhan's interventions, which represent knowledge based on more traditional methods of familial transmission. Through a variety of techniques, Siobhan attempts to reassert herself as a custodian of memory that is in the process of being compromised. Besides the use of word-based languages, she makes me look ridiculous through unflattering camera angles and twitchy edits that betray the number of 'takes' a scene required. These are reinforced by my own apparent insincerity and choice of performance clichés (like connecting the birth marks on my arms with a marker pen to literally map journeys on my body).

In fact, everything in the video that appeared to be most 'authentic' was not. For instance, the subtitles were not *really* Siobhan's 'voice'; we wrote and placed them together. Furthermore, the

The site of the text: Dee's tree. Photo courtesy of Dee Heddon.

one line I spoke that was not in Dee's original text (with the exception of reading the directions that she wrote in order to help us to find her tree over the opening credits), was rehearsed and performed more than any other in the film until it appeared to be spontaneous (unlike all the others). It was the line in which I realize that 'my square foot', the one in which I performed the first part of the script, was not in front of Dee's tree at all; in fact, it wasn't even a Sequoia. Siobhan and I were absolutely convinced that it would be impossible for anybody watching the film to associate my body and voice with the personal memories I recount in it, not least because my accent is evidently not Scottish. We were wrong.

It came as a complete surprise that many of the people who have watched our version of *Tree* in my company believed (at least from 'time to time' according to one audience member) that the speaking 'I' of the video was directly referring to my own personal history. These included people who had known me, although perhaps not especially well, for many years; above and beyond all the other planted clues in the video, they knew that my name was not Dee. It is perhaps also significant that those who were most able to recognize the rupture between 'me' and the 'I' of the spoken narrative, found the video quite funny (not unlike myself, Siobhan

Screenshot from *Tree*, made by Roberta Mock and Siobhan Mckeown (digital video, 2007).

and, eventually, Dee when she saw it) and this in itself troubled us even as we courted such a response.

In Carl Lavery's essay in this book, he discusses some of the ethical problems involved in the production of autobiographical performance. In making *Tree*, and presenting it to others, I was forced (somewhat unexpectedly) to encounter all those he outlines and a few more besides. 'The issue,' Carl writes, 'does not concern fabrication as such (we are, after all, speaking about performance), but, rather, the performer's capacity for respecting the privacy – the singularity – of the other'. For us, the issue *did* revolve around fabrication to some extent, especially as it related to that singularity. At various points Siobhan and I were deeply worried about whether we could be seen to be laughing at (or unfairly representing) Dee, her family, our family, our audiences, and even each other.

If the performance of *Tree* offered a more acute and nuanced understanding of the ethical implications of autobiographical performance, it also revealed to me some of its more formal elements. One of these is the use of 'listing' which, while by no means buried in the written text, rises to the surface through recitation.[33] In Dee's text, she makes it clear that we learn who/where we are, and how to communicate this interrelationship, by means of listing: 'I read somewhere that children in Scotland used to be taught their alphabet by listing trees rather than letters. A = Ailm, Elm; B = Beith, Birch; C = Coll, Hazel; D = Darrach, Oak; S = Seileach, Stewart; A = Ailm, Andrew; D = Darrach, Dee.'

In *Mourning Walk*, Carl tells us that 'Five Laverys have been killed in Northern Ireland since 1969: John Lavery (1971), John Lavery (1991), Martin Lavery (1974), Martin Lavery (1992) and Sean Lavery (no date).' Carl's performative act of listing, of organizing knowledge and experience subjectively, quickly extends to the representation of place. For instance, his list of plants, soon after the list of the Ulster dead who share his surname, is described as a 'botanical map' of his journey. Later, Carl consecutively lists the names of people and places that remind him of his father. Phil's lists are somewhat different; they can, perhaps, be best recognized as the overarching structure of his performance texts. He refers to the items he lists – the gossip, the myth, the history, the memories – as layers. By walking like a crab, he'd 'found all these layers – the gulls, the giant's eyes, the shifting sands of ghost houses, the Christmas trees under the Marram grass, the Neanderthal under Babbacombe'.

In performing *Tree* I never tried to be Dee and yet I was never not her. I borrowed from what might be considered non-representational styles of performing (for instance, by imagining that I was the presenter of a documentary). I tried to be myself (although not a particularly likeable version) within the confines of Dee's words rather than to embody them. In doing so, I thought a lot about my own childhood and its suburban landscape. And while there were no 'magic if's at work in my 'technique', I suspect this is at the heart of why so many audience members seem able to suspend their disbelief against all odds. In speaking Dee's memories, I conjured my own memories and those of my family – who also were forced to make long trips and give up their homes in order to survive – and while doing so, my material body was firmly located in the site from which these specific words and the memories they describe arose. Without realizing it at the time, I discovered what it meant to perform (like) myself. This, together with the insertion of my own childhood photographs and my daughter's presence, probably make the film as a whole very 'real' indeed. In retrospect, it seems obvious that what should have surprised me most was not that anybody did 'believe' me but that they did not since, with Dee and Siobhan, I did indeed create my own very revealing autobiographical performance text. 'You can find or make a route, my story in your story. Your life is not yours alone.'

There was another reason why I chose Dee's text to perform. In 2002, she 'followed in the footsteps' of Mike Pearson and reconstructed his autobiographical walking performance, *Bubbling Tom*. Although our approaches initially appear quite different, many commonalities can be recognized in our acts of creative interpretation: we both considered the original site to be a custodian and agent of memory; we both interpreted live performances we had not seen and refused to watch the 'originals' first on video; we both involved people with whom we are very close in the making of our new performances; we both misidentified or couldn't find the original sites of performance (and this was perhaps more productive and revealing than had we done so); we both encountered gaps in the score or text which needed to be filled; we both filled them with our own autobiographical memories. In reflecting upon her experience, Dee writes:

> As Pearson discovered, our interactions with place (alongside our various experiences of childhood) are often not as individual as we might imagine. He did this here. I did this here. This reminds me of what I did there. We did that too. I did nothing like that, but I did do this instead ...[34]

I hope you find the autobiographical texts in this book – both the plays and the essays that accompany them – as inspirational as I do. I hope they help you to unearth your own stories. I hope you make a walk. I hope you make a text. I hope you perform it to others. I hope you inspire others to do the same. It's really all about us.

Notes

1. Will Self, 'PsychoGeography. Motorway Madness', in *The Independent Magazine*, 25 February 2006.
2. Hamish Fulton, *Walking Artist* (Düsseldorf: Richter, 2001), p. 12.
3. The Site/Sight <=> Source/Resource Symposium took place on 11 and 12 September 2004, organized by Dee Heddon, Stephen Hodge and Les du S. Read. The programme is archived [online] http://www.people.ex.ac.uk/shodge/sitesymposium/introduction.html.
4. Indeed, in Detroit itself, from 2003–06, Walk & Squawk artists Erika Block and Hilary Ramsden led a series of events that focused on walking, performance, mapping, communities and cultural exchange. The Walking Project explored 'desire lines', or the 'unofficial' paths made by people who walk across fields or vacant lots. See [online] http://walksquawk.blogs.com/about_the_walking_project/.
5. Francesco Careri, *Walkscapes: Walking as an Aesthetic Practice* (Barcelona: Editorial Gustavo Gili, 2002), p. 170.

6. Smithson qtd in Careri, *Walkscapes*, p. 173.

7. Andreas Huyssen, 'Trauma and Memory: A New Imaginary of Temporality', in Jill Bennett and Roseanne Kennedy (eds), *World Memory: Personal Trajectories in Global Time* (London: Palgrave Macmillan, 2003), p. 28.

8. Mieke Bal, 'Introduction', in Mieke Bal, Jonathan Crewe and Leo Spitzer (eds) *Acts of Memory: Cultural Recall in the Present* (Hanover: University Press of New England, 1999), p. xi.

9. Deirdre Heddon, *Autobiography and Performance* (London: Palgrave Macmillan, 2008), pp. 106–07, 109.

10. Svetlana Boym, *The Future of Nostalgia* (New York: Basic Books, 2001), p. 49.

11. Heddon, *Autobiography and Performance*, p. 92.

12. Careri, *Walkscapes*, pp. 166, 168.

13. Phil Smith, 'Dread, Route and Time: An Autobiographical Walking of Everything Else', *Reconstruction*, 3(1), Winter 2003 [online] http://reconstruction.eserver.org/031/smith.htm.

14. There are two other relevant observations to make about my 'home'. The first is that it was actually located in a suburb of a city (Windsor, Ontario, Canada) that many consider to be a suburb of Detroit itself (thus, I grew up in a suburb of a suburb that was oddly closer in distance to the city of Detroit than most of its other suburbs). And secondly, it was actually *in* downtown Detroit – if not more than in its suburbs, then more surprisingly and dramatically – that such post-industrial wastelands were to be found. I spent many hours with friends who were visual artists, absorbing the atmospheres of crumbling buildings while they photographed Detroit's inner-city 'monuments'. This impulse is documented on the *Fabulous Ruins of Detroit* website [online] http://detroityes.com/home.htm. Not unrelated, it could also be noted that while Smithson was preparing his *Monuments* exhibition and article in the summer of 1967, the cities of Newark (located just south of Passaic, also on the Passaic River) and Detroit were burning. Detroit never recovered financially, materially or culturally from the riots that lasted five days and left 43 people dead. See *Riots 1967* [online] http://www.67riots.rutgers.edu/.

15. Peggy Phelan, *Mourning Sex* (London: Routledge, 1997), pp. 11–12.

16. Careri, *Walkscapes*, p. 157.

17. Laura Marcus, *Auto/biographical Discourses: Theory, Criticism, Practice* (Manchester: Manchester University Press, 1994), p. 287.

18. Doreen Massey, *For Space* (London: Sage Publications, 2005), p. 24.

19. Mike Pearson, *'In Comes I': Performance, Memory and Landscape* (Exeter: Exeter University Press, 2006), p. 12.

20. Nancy K. Miller, *Getting Personal* (London & New York: Routledge, 1991), p. 24.

21. As I have stated elsewhere, I consider these dialogic processes to be fundamental to live performance. See Roberta Mock, 'Introduction', in Roberta Mock (ed.), *Performing Processes: Creating Live Performance* (Bristol: Intellect, 2000).

22. Deirdre Heddon, 'Performing Lesbians: Constructing the Self, Constructing the Community', in Maggie B. Gale and Viv Gardner (eds), *Auto/biography and Identity: Women, Theatre and Performance* (Manchester & New York: Manchester University Press, 2004), pp. 229, 238.

23. Dwight Conquergood, 'Performance Studies: Interventions and Radical Research', in Henry Bial (ed.), *The Performance Studies Reader* (London & New York: Routledge, 2004), p. 376.

24. Brian Massumi interview, 'Navigating Movements', 2002, pp. 10–11 [online] http://www.brianmassumi.com/interviews/NAVIGATING%20MOVEMENTS.pdf.

25. ibid., p. 3.

26. See, for instance, Mike Pearson, 'Bubbling Tom', in Adrian Heathfield (ed.) *Small Acts: Performance, the Millennium and the Marking of Time* (London: Black Dog Publishing, 2000); or Claudia Wegener, 'Manresa: Autobiography as Method...', *Performance Research*, 7(3), 2002, pp. 30–46 and continued in 8(2), 2003, pp. 117–34.

27. Shirley Neuman, 'Autobiography: From Different Poetics to a Poetics of Differences', in Marlene Kadar (ed.), *Essays on Life Writing: From Genre to Critical Practice* (Toronto: University of Toronto Press, 1992), p. 214.

28. Although I'm still unable to answer the questions in the preceding paragraph in any generic sense, I did confirm their personal value as a starting point for reflexive performance practice-as-research processes.

29. I have briefly discussed this, as well as the move from site-based devising to theatrical staging, in relation to Lusty Juventus's *M(other) Project*. See Roberta Mock, 'Birth of Character/Death of Director' [online] http://www.lustyjuventus.co.uk/BCDD.html.

30. All of Dee's performances and processes, indoors and outdoors, were documented on video by Peter Hulton. See *One Square Foot: An Exploration into Interdisciplinary Performer Training*, DVD-Rom (Exeter: Arts Documentation Unit, 2004). Although Peter was kind enough to provide me with a copy, I only watched the studio performance long enough to discover how to pronounce the Gaelic words. I was worried that I would otherwise start imitating Dee in performance.

31. Dan Rebellato, 'Playwriting and Globalization: Towards a Site-Unspecific Theatre', *Contemporary Theatre Review*, 16(1), 2006, p. 113.

32. *Tree*, digital video, 12 minutes. Directed and edited by Siobhan Mckeown. Performed by Roberta Mock. Spoken text by Dee Heddon. First screened to the Performance and the Body Working Group at the Theatre & Performance Research Association (TaPRA) conference, University of Birmingham, September 2007. An excerpt can be viewed [online] http://www.youtube.com/watch?v=PE8FP6L 19S8&feature=user. *Tree* was conceived as a practice-as-research project and a more aesthetically driven version for non-academic audiences is in the process of being edited.

33. Many others have noted the close relationship between listing and autobiography. In 2006, Lisa Nola and Adam Marks launched the Listography Project, which offers formats (including websites and books) through which readers can shape and share their own autobiographies by making personal lists. See http://listography.com.

34. Deirdre Heddon, 'Performing the Archive: Following in the Footsteps', *Performance Research: On Archives*, 7(4), 2002, p. 185.

PART 1: CARL LAVERY

MOURNING WALK

by Carl Lavery

Performed at Lancaster University, December 2006
Lighting: Stephanie Sims

and Nuffield Theatre, Lancaster, 1 March 2008

In performance, all text is spoken except the lines in bold in the box at the very start of the script. The dates that run throughout the piece serve to mark shifts in direction. They are usually followed by a lengthy pause. Images are similarly projected on a screen behind me. Unlike in the written text, they have a sense of duration, and last as long as I see fit. All the images were taken during my walk. However, in the live performance, I also use additional images such as found photographs of artists and thinkers whose lines are cited in the text. Thank you to Nick Strong for helping to prepare these images for publication. (CL)

Mourning Walk: 29.07.04

Market Harborough to Cottesmore

Lane – Field – Road

18 miles

On 29 July 2004, to mark the ninth anniversary of my Dad's death, I walked eighteen miles as the crow flies from the town of Market Harborough in Leicestershire to the village of Cottesmore in Lincolnshire. At the end of the journey I performed a ritual in a field. I have nothing to say about that. Certain things ought to be kept secret.

October 1981

In Autumn 1981 my Dad spent ten weeks at an RAF camp in Cottesmore. He was on a course, learning how to fix Tornado fighter planes – the newest form of military jet. He used to work on Phantoms. Once he came home with a MacDonald Douglas holdall bag that an American pilot had left behind in the cockpit. He was very proud of it, and we were impressed. We'd seen nothing like this before. It looked great. Green silk; lightweight; pure style.

But today, I'm sitting at a table trying to do my French homework. I'm bored – I don't get this. I look over at the table and see my father working at something himself. He's got a pen, a geometry set and a calculator – and it looks like he's thinking. This is strange; I'm not used to it. I guess this is what he does at Cottesmore. He seems to like it. Normally, when he comes home from work he's tired and wants to sleep before he makes dinner. My mother only cooks on the weekend. She works in the NAAFI shop at St Athan and doesn't finish work until 6 p.m. On Wednesday afternoons, I stop in and see her at work. I have a job delivering papers to the Officers' mess. She's always pleased to see me and often buys me a chocolate bar. My presence breaks the routine. My Mum hates her job. There's nothing strange about that. Everybody I know hates working on the camp.

According to an American poet:

The chain of memory is resurrection
The vector of space is resurrection
Direction is resurrection
Time is the face of recognition.[1]

I chose this walk after reconstructing my Dad's journey with the help of my Mum. We think he probably took the M4 from Cardiff to Bristol; the M5 from Bristol to Worcester; the A46 from Worcester to Leamington Spa; the A426 from Leamington to Lutterworth; the A4304 from Lutterworth to Market Harborough via Husband's Bosworth; the A6003 from Market Harborough to Oakham; and finally the B668 from Oakham to Cottesmore.

Although I wasn't following the route exactly – the road from Market Harbrough to Oakham is a busy A road – this didn't bother me unduly. My mum had told me that he liked the countryside between Market Harborough and Oakham, and I imagined him on a Friday afternoon driving through the gentle Wolds of the Welland Valley. He always said that work was an inconvenience between weekends.

October 1994

It's a dog day today – one of the last in an Indian summer – and my Dad's taken the day off work to drive me and Melanie, my wife, through the South Wales valleys to Hay-on-Wye to visit the second-hand bookshops. I buy *The Confederacy of Dunces* by John Kennedy Toole and something on psychoanalysis. We have lunch and a pint in a pub. Later that night, we watch Aston Villa beat Inter Milan on ITV. I wonder if he knew that he was ill as he walked around Hay.

Saturday, 29 July 1995

My father died at home, in his bed, at about 7.30 a.m. on the hottest day of a hot summer. When I walk to town to buy food for lunch later that day, my trousers stick to my leg. I've never experienced heat like this before in Britain. I don't want to move and the sun is hurting my eyes. I feel sick. I'm at the junction of Stalcourt Avenue and the Beach Road. I can see the comprehensive school – the one I went to – in the distance. It's about 200 yards away. Melanie's with me – she's wearing a dress straight out of the 1950s. It's got big red and green flowers on it. We're both hot, we're both shocked, we both feel unreal. My Dad's gone – they took his body out of the house this morning. Because of the heat, I never see his face again. We buried him on a Friday.

Wednesday, 29 July 2004

Melanie and my son Immanuel drive me to a village just north of Market Harborough. This is where I start my walk. It's a hot day – the hottest day of a wet summer. I feel relieved to get started. The thought of doing the walk has made me anxious for the past week, and I've begun to suffer from insomnia again, waking at 4 a.m. But today the sun is in the sky; the wheat is in the field; and the light is strong. And I'm wishing I had more of a language for landscape.

If I am walking, I almost physically feel the current of time slowing down in the gravitational field of oblivion. It seems to me then as if all the moments of our life occupy the same space, as if future events already existed and were only waiting for us to find our way to them at last, just as when we have accepted an invitation we duly arrive in a certain house at a given time. And might it not be that we also have an appointment to keep in the past, in what has gone before and is for the most part extinguished, and must go there in search of places and people who have some connection with us on the far side of time, so to speak?[2]

The land between Market Harborough and Cottesmore dates from the Jurassic period, a layer of rock that runs invisibly through the centre of England from Dorset to East Yorkshire.

A geological mapping of the route: Market Harborough – Lower Jurassic – Clay/Silt; Medbourne – Marlstone Rockbed/Lower Lias; Oakham – Middle Jurassic – Inferior Oolite; Cottesmore – Lower Lincolnshire Limestone.

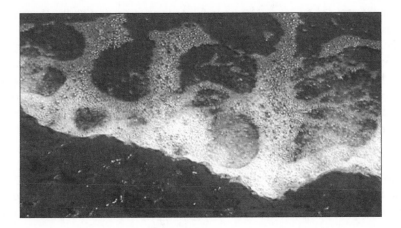

The Welland River marks the county boundary between Northamptonshire and Leicestershire. From there, the Welland runs to the Wash, and then into the North Sea. This is important for me. I've always lived by the coast, and feel landlocked in the Midlands. When a dreamer of reveries has swept aside all the preoccupations which were encumbering his everyday life, when he has detached himself from the worry which comes to him from the worry of others, when he is truly the author of his solitude, that dreamer feels that time is suspended. There is no longer any yesterday and no tomorrow. Time is engulfed in the double depth of the dreamer and the world.[3] Walking is a technique of solitude, a way into reverie. The walker is not a sleepwalker but a daydreamer. There's a crucial difference here that demands attention. The sleepwalker is dead to the world; he has no engagement with it; he's immersed in the unconsciousness of sleep. The daydreamer by contrast is alive to the environment, and recreates it through his imagination. He's open to the shock of things. When I walk, I go back and forth in an infinite journey between memory and imagination.

Summer 1972

I'm sitting on the steps of a terraced house in Glencolyer Street, just off the Limestone Road in South Belfast. The 'Troubles' are all around me, all in me, but I don't know that yet. My Mum's in the kitchen with my new baby brother, Gareth. I'm waiting for my Dad to come home from work. I'm expectant – it's his payday and he always brings me a comic. He arrives. I'm happy. He runs his hand through my hair and I smell the leather on his jacket. He gives me the comic. I look at it and reject it. It's not the one I want. There's an immediate change of atmosphere. He takes the comic back, and tells me that I'm getting nothing. I panic. I change my mind. I do want it, after all. But it's too late. It's gone. I never see that comic. And to this day, I don't know what it was. This was my first lesson in disappointment.

December 2005: After the Walk

I'm looking for something on landscape in the journal *Performance Research*. I scan the page of contents on the back cover of a 1997 volume called *Letters from Europe*, and start to look for two articles, 'From Logos to Landscape: Text in Contemporary Dramaturgy' and 'Text as Landscape'. As I do so, I come across, quite by chance, a contribution from the Northern Irish artist Alistair MacLennan in the section of the journal that deals with contributions from artists and creative writers.[4] His piece is called 'MAEL 69/96 to Commemorate All Those Killed As a Result of the Northern Irish Troubles'. The tribute is simple and minimalist. It reminds me of the Vietnam War memorial in Washington D.C. On the top left-hand column of the left-hand page, there is a thumbnail image of a dead bird, quite possibly a swallow. The rest of the eight pages then list in alphabetical order the names of those killed in the 'Troubles'. I pay particular attention when I get to the letter L, and more specifically to the name Lavery. Five Laverys have been killed in Northern Ireland since 1969: John Lavery (1971), John Lavery (1991), Martin Lavery (1974), Martin Lavery (1992) and Sean Lavery (no date).

The name Lavery is an old Ulster name and crosses the sectarian divide. But, with the exception of Sean Lavery, all the Laverys listed in MacLellan's monument have a Protestant ring to them. The Christian names are the give away. I wonder, as I read these names, what would have happened to my family if we had stayed in Belfast and not moved to Llantwit Major in 1976. I also wonder if I'm related to any of the dead.

Unlike my Mum who suffered from it, my Dad, as far as I know, was never homesick for Northern Ireland. He seemed to have no attachment to the place, although he did run around the garden once when Northern Ireland beat Spain in Seville during the 1982 World Cup.

A botanical map of my journey:

Fox Glove, Milk Thistle, Borridge, Dandelion, Dog-Rose, Bracken, Furze, Ling, Tussock Grass, Violet, Meadow-rue, Bird's Foot Trefoil, Burnet, Sorrel, Gentian, Meadow Saxifrage, Clover, Hay-rattle, Rock-Rose, Buttercup, Cuckoo-Flower, Ragged Robin, Self-Heal.

August 1992

I'm coming down the stairs at home sometime in the late morning. My parents have just come back from Greece, and my brother is getting a bollocking. He's forgotten to water my Dad's tomato plants – and he's 'killed a bumper crop'. Melanie is still in bed asleep. When I tell her about it she laughs. The phrase 'a bumper crop' became a comic memory for my family, and on the night my father died, we laughed about it again, trying to keep him alive in language and memory.

June 1995

My dad was diagnosed with cancer in early June 1995, about a week after my birthday, which falls on 31 May – the same day as Clint Eastwood's. Melanie had bought me a new pair of shoes as a present. I remember throwing them from the upstairs window into the garden. I think it was a Monday. At the time, I was tutoring X, which meant I had to wait until Friday before we could go and visit my Dad. Melanie had to arrange to get time off work too. Anyway, I remember that we took the train from Norwich to Wales on a Friday. It was unseasonably cold when we left Norwich. I left the gas on. When we returned from Wales the following week, I was surprised to see a small blue flame rising from the white bars of the fire.

Because my Dad was in the hospital, my Mum picked us up from the station. The next day was the start of the heat wave which was to last throughout the summer. My Dad was in bed when we arrived at the hospital and he complimented me on a new shirt I'd bought from a charity shop in Norwich. After some random testing, he was discharged from hospital and drove the car back in a very impatient and tense way. This was uncharacteristic; he was normally a careful driver who didn't like to waste fuel. In the afternoon, we watched the Rugby World Cup on TV. He told me off for smoking too much. I told him I was stressed. He nodded and agreed. We talked around the subject of his not being there.

My Dad went back to hospital on Sunday night for more checks. I noticed that he didn't eat anything before he left. The next day, the Monday, we drive to the hospital to see him. He seems frail, but the weight loss means that he looks younger. Almost the way I remember him when I was a child, and he was in his early 20s and looked a bit like Rod Stewart. He walks with us to the hospital doors. Melanie and my Mum are ahead of me – they are almost at the car. I turn around, and watch my Dad walk back into the hospital, alone. This image, an image that somehow for me captures the very essence of loneliness, will continue to haunt me. As I write, I can't get Kafka's short story 'Before the Law' out of my head. I think of the incident in the story when the gatekeeper tells the protagonist that the door he has been endlessly waiting to open is his own unique door. Nobody else can walk through it. Until now that memory has stayed within me, hidden deep in my own private space. And even now as I speak of it, I'm sure of having failed to communicate its real sense.

I feel there is much to be said for the Celtic belief that the souls of those whom we have lost are held captive in some inferior being, in an animal, in a plant, in some inanimate object, and thus effectively lost to us until the day (which to many never comes) when we happen to pass by the tree or to obtain possession of the object which forms their prison. Then they start to tremble and they call us by our name, and as soon as we recognise their voice the spell is broken. Delivered by us, they have overcome death and return to share our life.

'And so it is with our own past. It is a labour in vain to attempt to recapture it: all the efforts of our intellect must prove futile. The past is hidden somewhere outside the realm, beyond the reach of intellect, in some hidden object... of which we have no inkling. And it depends on chance whether or not we come upon this object before we ourselves must die.'[5]

Due no doubt to having spent most of my formative years in the countryside, nature, for me, is always associated with childhood. And that's probably why it calms me down so much. It seems to hold out the possibility of happiness, some sense of completion. On my walk to Cottesmore, I was on the lookout for frogs. I remember once playing on a boggy heath in Antrim. The ponds that covered the landscape were thick and full of spawn. I took some home and watched it turn into tadpoles and then into frogs. My Mum didn't know what to do with a bucket of baby frogs and flushed them down the toilet. Frogspawn fascinates me because it's material for change. I liked the tadpoles best when they were at their most monstrous with little legs, arms and tails.

The relationship between the idea for a walk, the walk itself and the physical evidence of the walk is the fundamental issue. The idea is vital in that it defines the structure for a walk. But the walk is equally important in that it realises the idea, actualising the structure as physical movement through time and space so that the work of art has a *real* – if transient – existence.[6]

August 1974

We've just moved to Antrim from Belfast. The 1974 World Cup is over and I have vague memories of Holland playing Germany in the final. I like the orange jerseys worn by the Dutch. Because my parents are young and have little spare cash, we always go out exploring in the summer evenings. We walk everywhere and go quite far, heading for the hills in the distance. Often I'm so tired they have to take my brother out of the pram and put me in it. I am too heavy to carry. One particular evening comes to mind. It is high summer, and the light is still strong. Summer nights in Ulster are long and seem to last forever. We walk through a field of flowers and come across a farmhouse recently abandoned. Everything is still in place and there are boxes and tins everywhere. There's also an Aga and milk churns. My Dad took some light-fittings from the wall. We returned to the farmhouse in Spring and it was full of flowers.

Names I associate with my Dad: Duncairn, Limestone, Glencolyer, Stiles Farm, Six Mile Water, Bellevue, Crawshay, Manor Park, Beach Road, Ogmore.

Other names I associate with my Dad: John Wayne, Audie Murphy, Cochise, Geronimo, Chief Scar, Louis L'Amour, Valdez, Burt Lancaster, Sitting Bull, General Custer, Little Big Horn, Sioux, Apache, Davy Crockett.

From this walk I bring back words, rhythm, and flecks of pollen from my path through the bee-field. The Jurassic way is a pre-historic pathway, 300 miles in length, that runs from the South-West to the North-East of England. You get some sense of the history of the path by following the stretch of Green Lane that runs from Belton to Oakham. This was a drover's path. No one walks on it now.

I asked my Mum for a photograph of my Dad taken as he was watching a phantom take off from a runway in St Athan. It's a bright summer's day and he's on top of a hangar, wearing a pair of green work overalls. The photograph has been lost, apparently. My Mum lent it to one of my Dad's workmates and he never returned it. I reconstruct the photograph from my memory. It's not difficult to do. As I remember it, the photograph shows my Dad watching and not watching at the same time. He appears to be looking at the jet he's just fixed, and he's smiling. A naïve reading would say that he's proud of his work, and I suppose that's why the picture was taken: to mark a job well done. But this is to miss the point somewhat. My Dad is not really interested in the plane; his gaze is elsewhere. He's staring into the sky and escaping from everything – from work, from home, from us, from himself. He's dreaming and appears content.

'If learning to live remains to be done, it can happen only between life and death. Neither in life nor in death *alone* but between the two. So it would be necessary then to learn how to speak with or about ghosts. Especially since, the spectre *is not*, and never present *as such*. The time of the "learning to live" would amount to this: to live otherwise and better in the companionship of ghosts. No not better, but more justly. But with them. No being-with the other, no *socius* without the absence, the presence, of the ghost. And this being with spectres would be a politics of memory, of inheritance, and of generation.'[7]

My son Immanuel was born five years after my Dad died. When I look at him, I see my Dad. It's hard to say where the resemblance is exactly, but it's there. And it comes from his face. I'm sure of that.

Most of the memories I've talked about here are good memories. They won't offend anyone, and the walk through Leicestershire allowed me to rediscover them as if in a trough of time. I'm aware that I've said nothing of the bad days, the days when it all went wrong. That's because those memories call out for a different language, a language where you can hide yourself in others – a language, perhaps, for actors on a stage.

Notes

1. Charles Olson, 'The Chain of Memory is Resurrection', in *Charles Olson: Selected Poems* (Berkeley: The University of California Press, 1993), pp. 65–66.
2. W.G. Sebald, *Austerlitz* (London: Penguin Books, 2002), p. 360.
3. Gaston Bachelard, *The Poetics of Reverie: Childhood, Language and the Cosmos* (Boston: Beacon Press, 1991), p. 174.
4. Alistair MacLennan, 'MAEL 69/96 to Commemorate All Those Killed As a Result of the Northern Irish Troubles', *Performance Research,* 2:1 (1997), pp. 92–99.
5. Marcel Proust, *Remembrance of Things Past,* vol. 1 (London: Penguin, 1984), pp. 47–48.
6. Paul Moorhouse, *Richard Long: Walking the Line* (London: Thames & Hudson, 2002), p. 16.
7. Jacques Derrida, *Specters of Marx: The State of the Debt, The Work of Mourning, and The New International* (New York & London: Routledge, 1994), p. xviii.

Mourning Walk and Pedestrian Performance: History, Aesthetics and Ethics

Carl Lavery

Preparing the Ground

In early November 2005, two e-mail messages 'pinged' my inbox within five minutes of each other. The first was from Gordon Ramsay in the Theatre Department at the University of Nottingham inviting me to talk about walking as performance to his MA students; the second was from Martin Hargreaves, editor of *Dance Theatre Journal*, informing me that *Electric Walk*, the latest work from the German artist Christina Kubisch, was to be installed on Kensington High Street from November to December 2005. For some time, I had been agonizing over how best to write an essay that would place *Mourning Walk* within the fields of walking, autobiography and performance. In a somewhat fraught context (the deadline was fast approaching and my wife was due to give birth to our second child), the e-mails sent by Gordon and Martin seemed to work according to the Surrealist law of 'objective chance'. Inadvertently, they had unearthed a magnetic field of inspiration and provided me with the imaginative spark – the *déclic* – required to set about my task. It soon became clear that this essay needed to address two issues. First, it had to map the territory of pedestrian performance in general, and then use that map to situate my own practice within the larger context of contemporary performance. Second, it needed to deal with notions of enchantment, reverie and healing, and, at the same time, to explore what might be called the aesthetics and ethics of autobiographical performance.

What follows below is my attempt to fulfil these objectives, which came to me suddenly and fortuitously through an innocent exchange of e-mails. Using the logic of objective chance as the catalyst for this essay is more than mere whimsy however, for this is exactly what the Surrealists (and to a lesser extent the situationists) did as they wandered errantly and aimlessly through the hidden gardens and labyrinthine arcades of the city. With them, as for me, walking and writing are intimately connected: one leads to the other.

Walking and Performance: A Brief Literature Review

In *Wanderlust: A Short History of Walking* (2001), Rebecca Solnit claims that the origin of the current vogue for pedestrian performance art can be traced to Amsterdam in the early 1960s when Stanley Brouwn, a Dutch emigré from Surinam, 'asked strangers on the street to draw him directions or locations around town and exhibited the results as a vernacular art of encounters or a collection of drawings'.[1] In the final chapter of her book, 'The Shape of a Walk', Solnit uses this event as a launching pad to explore the role of walking in the work of avant-garde performance artists such as Robert Smithson, Carolee Schneemann, Vito Acconci, Sophie Calle, and Marina Abramovic and Ulay. According to Solnit, the relationship between walking and avant-garde performance practice is a natural one. For if avant-garde art is concerned, as the performance theorist Allan Kaprow maintained, with undoing rigid distinctions between art and life, then what could be more effective for achieving this collapse than proclaiming a walk through the city to be a performance in its own right?:

> For the artists who took up the invitation Kaprow outlined, art ceased to be a craft-based discipline of making objects and became a kind of unbounded investigation into the relationship between ideas, acts, and the material world. At a time when the institutions of galleries and museums and the objects made for them seemed moribund, this new conceptual and dematerialized art sought a new arena and a new immediacy for artmaking. Art objects might be only the evidence of such an investigation or props or prompts for the viewers' own investigations, while artists could model themselves after scientists, shamans, detectives, or philosophers as they expanded the possible repertoire of gestures far beyond that of the painter at his canvas [...]. In retrospect, it seems as though these artists were remaking the world, act by act, object by object, starting with the simplest substances, shapes, gestures. One such gesture – an ordinary one from which the extraordinary can be derived – is walking.[2]

Solnit's study of walking and performance in the penultimate chapter of *Wanderlust*, although admirably accessible, is nevertheless largely derivative – most of it, for instance, is based on the American art critic Lucy Lippard's text, *Overlay: Contemporary Art and the Art of Prehistory* (1993).[3]

A more original approach to walking and performance is found in *Theatre/Archaeology* (2001) by Mike Pearson and Michael Shanks. Where Solnit's text concentrates on walking and performance art, Pearson and Shanks prefer to focus on the relationship between walking and various forms of site-specific theatre. The book is highly experimental in form and structure and sets up a series of dialogues between theories of walking, concepts of archaeology and landscape, and extracts from Pearson's work with the Welsh-based company Brith Gof, and, more recently, Mike Brookes.

In their discussion of walking in the city, Pearson and Shanks list four types of pedestrian performer, each of whom is linked to a key cultural theorist: the walker, the *flâneur*, the nomad and the rambler. In their typology, the walker is defined in terms of Michel de Certeau's notion of the 'user' of the city, an itinerant figure who escapes from the disciplinary grid (strategy) imposed by urban planners and architects by following his/her own desires, whims and inclinations (tactics). Endorsing de Certeau's argument, Pearson and Shanks claim that the errant 'desire paths' opened up by the pedestrian performer are ways of rewriting the city, of making place (the official meaning given to any environment) into space (the individual's idiosyncratic relationship with his/her environment). Paraphrasing de Certeau, Shanks and Pearson note:

> It is the pedestrians who transform the street into a space. Yet this walking is often orientated. We are drawn back to significant places, familiar places, memorable places, weaving them together in improvised narratives. We both read and write. Through memory and imagination, we can claim a measure of control.[4]

Pearson and Shanks are more circumspect about the political potential of their second pedestrian performer: the *flâneur*.

In the boulevards and arcades of nineteenth-century Paris, the city where, according to Walter Benjamin, the commodity first launched its assault on consciousness, the *flâneur* attempted to escape commodification by endlessly roaming the streets in a quest to track down what the Surrealists called 'le merveilleux' (the marvellous). For Benjamin, the Messianic Marxist, the *flâneur*'s peregrinations through the public space of the city had the ability to redeem the world from reification by positing the urban as a site of play and theatre, and not as a utilitarian zone of exchange value. Writing in an age of shopping malls and digital advertisement, Pearson and Shanks are less optimistic about the *flâneur*'s capacity for redemption:

> With the advent of the modern city, the concept of the *flâneur* has come to stand as a metaphor for the contemporary urban dweller, moving through the flux of the city, as a mode of being in the world, in relation to the dazzling consumer spectacles: in a modern shopping centre we are all *flâneurs*: gazing, grazing, consuming.[5]

Shanks and Pearson have more faith in their third pedestrian performer: the nomad. Where today's *flâneur*, they believe, is seduced by a dazzling display of visual information in the city and is thus reduced to a passive bystander, a mere consumer of images, the nomad refuses to stop and look, preferring instead the bodily joys of constant motion and dynamic flux.

In keeping with the theories of Gilles Deleuze and Félix Guattari, the originators of the term 'nomodology' in *A Thousand Plateaus: Capitalism and Schizophrenia, Vol.2*, the nomadic walker sees the city as a boundless stage where the self can be sacrificed and shattered, and where new ecstatic intensities can be experienced. For Shanks and Pearson, the performance of the nomad is inherently political; s/he destabilizes the disciplinary structures that fix and regulate the city's identity:

The nomad shifts across the smooth space of the urban desert using points and locations to define paths rather than places to be, making the most of circumstance. The enemy of the nomad is the state, which wants to take the space and enclose it and to create fixed identities and well-directed paths for movement. And the nomad, cut free of roots, bonds and identities, is the enemy of the state, resisting its discipline.[6]

Shanks and Pearson conclude their set of pedestrian performance practices by referring to Jane Rendell's 'rambler', an urban walker who 'rethinks the city as a series of paces or flows of movement, in pursuit of pleasure: moving between the sites of leisure, pleasure, consumption, exchange and display'.[7] However, unlike the 'walker' or 'nomad', the pedestrian performance of the rambler, according to Rendell, offers neither political resistance nor ecstatic liberation. On the contrary, the rambler is a reactionary figure, a masculine predator who moves through the city voyeuristically consuming the images of femininity constantly on display. For Rendell, walking is yet another patriarchal attempt to control space by imprisoning women in confined places (the domestic, the supermarket, the brothel) where they can be placed under surveillance and disciplined.[8]

Theatre/Archaeology is the first study to explore in detail the function of walking in site-specific performance and theatre. One of the great strengths of the book is that performance and performativity are never, for all their similarities, elided into one.[9] Rather, Pearson and Shanks are sensitive to the differences involved in these activities. This allows them to offer a more accurate analysis of how *walking in performance* (as opposed to *walking as performance*) can draw attention to, and potentially disrupt, the spectacle of everyday life itself. However, despite the admirable emphasis it places on theatre practice, *Theatre/Archaeology* nevertheless relies too heavily on theory in its attempt to explain the current interest in site, space and place.[10] Although much is made of the economic hardships experienced in post-industrial Wales, there is no attempt in the book to explore the economic, technological and sociological factors that have increasingly led contemporary performance makers to focus on walking as a privileged mode of itinerant performance.

The film-maker and writer Patrick Keiller is one of the few commentators to have attempted to think through the relationship between theory and performance in terms other than critical theory. In his short essay 'Popular Science' published in the catalogue accompanying the visual art exhibition *Landscape* (2000), Keiller focuses on economic factors.[11] More specifically, he is interested in how the 'anomalous high cost of built structure' has resulted in a dearth of new architecture in the United Kingdom:

> In a context where building – not just the building of houses, but all building – has become more expensive, so that the volume of new construction is less than it used to be, new architecture has assumed a kind of scarcity value. It has become exotic, so that its representation and discussion in various media is now much more widespread than was the case when encounters with actual built architecture were more common.[12]

For Keiller, the new media discourse on architecture has played an important role in sensitizing individuals to their surroundings. However, the failure of contemporary urban planners to meet these new aesthetic expectations has caused United Kingdom city-dwellers to search for alternative methods of gratification. According to Keiller, they have primarily looked inward, towards the imagination:

> For most people, in most of the landscapes of 'advanced' economies, the transformation of everyday surroundings is achieved much less by physical buildings than by other means. [...] In the UK, the subjective transformation of landscape seems to offer the individual a way to oppose the poverty of everyday surroundings. As individuals we can't rebuild the public transport system or re-empower local democracy but we can poeticise our relationship with dilapidation.[13]

In Keiller's provocative thesis, pedestrian performance (what he sarcastically refers to as the 'UK's psychogeography phenomenon') is simultaneously an ingenious response to the poverty of urban living and a subjective attempt to withstand social and economic disempowerment. However, notwithstanding the very obvious political critique that Keiller carries out in films such as *London* (1994) and *Robinson in Space* (1997), it is difficult to say with any real certainty if he sees pedestrian performance in the essay 'Popular Science' as a form of popular resistance or as a gesture of defeat, a futile attempt to withstand alienation.[14]

Although he does not refer to performance practice *per se*, Keiller's explanation for the current vogue in psychogeography is certainly applicable to the contemporary breed of performance makers in the United Kingdom who take the city as their stage. Spectators are drawn to the work of Gob Squad and Lone Twin (amongst others) because they provide a mobile and potentially 'democratic' frame through which the complex interplay between performance and various forms of urban practice can be highlighted.[15] From this perspective, pedestrian performance – the fact that the audience has to share the same space and time as the performers – is a stimulus, a method for encouraging spectators to rewrite and imagine their own city.

It is important to stress here that site-specific pedestrian performance works very differently from more traditional forms of representing space, such as landscape poetry or psychogeographic writing. Whereas literature, as the writer and walker Iain Sinclair points out, functions to 'hold landscape, and its overwhelming, simultaneous particulars, in the float of memory',[16] pedestrian performance does the reverse. Its objective is to overwhelm us in the present, to provide us with actual experience, to make the world 'float' in the here and now. This is where pedestrian performance displays its avant-garde heritage: its ultimate purpose is to replace vicarious experience (reading someone else's account of space) with actual experience (producing one's own spatial map).[17]

Why Pedestrian Performance?

Keiller's explanation for the return of the poet-walker to U.K. cities is a welcome attempt to ground psychogeography in economic materialism. However, it is not enough by itself to account for the contemporary interest in walking and performance. The major difficulty with Keiller's thesis is that he has no way of explaining the unique type of aesthetic experience involved in site-specific pedestrianism. Audiences do not simply attend the work of companies such as Wrights & Sites or Lone Twin because they want to construct imaginary types of dream architecture, building projects in the mind. Rather they attend such events, I would argue, because they are looking for a particular form of aesthetic pleasure that is essentially unbounded, what the Canadian philosopher and aesthetician Allen Carlson terms 'environmental aesthetics'.[18] If it is agreed that 'environmental aesthetics', as Carlson intimates, are an ontological given, a feeling for natural beauty hardwired into the brain, then pedestrian performance transcends Keiller's attempt to place it within a precise historical and geographical framework.[19] Consequently it is important to look elsewhere for alternative explanations, particularly so when it is a question of understanding pedestrian performances, like NVA's *The Path* (2003) and *The Old Man of Storr* (2005), which are located in rural landscapes, and thus have little in common with Keiller's urban-based model of psychogeography.

A good place from which to start this enquiry is to focus on what we might call the 'Romantic-Humanist' approach to space. From this influential perspective, pedestrian performance is attractive to individuals because it allows them to re-discover a holistic relationship with place that contemporary spatial practices prevent. In this tradition – and the spectres of Jean-Jacques Rousseau, Henry David Thoreau and William Wordsworth loom large in it – pedestrian performance is an attempt to get beyond performance, a way of accessing 'authentic' human experience. The problem here, of course, as many spatial theorists have pointed out, is that there is no 'proper' relationship with space. Space is not a timeless substance in which the truth of the human subject is written; it is historically conditioned and dependent upon the performances that have given rise to it in the first place.[20] Accordingly, the value of pedestrian performance is not to be found in the way it supposedly unveils the truth of the world, but, on the contrary, for its ability to highlight the essentially performative quality of landscape. By doing so, pedestrian performance avoids the paradoxical narcissism so prevalent in the Romantic-Humanist approach to nature – that is to say, the process whereby the human ego finds itself reflected in its surroundings.

An alternative (but ultimately related) rationale for pedestrian performance is articulated by contemporary French sociologists and ethnographers such as Marc Augé and Paul Virilio. According to them, the contemporary obsession with speed and dynamic mobility has rendered the world placeless, a kind of virtual desert. As Augé puts it:

> In one form or another, ranging from the misery of refugee camps to the cosseted luxury of five-star hotels, some experience of non-place (indissociable from a more or less clear perception of the acceleration of history and the contraction of the planet) is today an essential component of all social existence.[21]

Viewed from the position of what Virilio in *Speed and Politics: An Essay on Dromology* (1986) calls 'dromology' (the science of speed), pedestrian performance is a mode of resistance against the acceleration of the world, a desire, on the part of performance makers, to rehumanize space by encouraging spectators to experience the environment at a properly human pace, the bodily beat of three miles per hour. Implicit in this argument is the belief that walking is conducive to the production of place, a perfect technique for merging landscape, memory and imagination in a dynamic dialogue. Or as Michel de Certeau would have it: 'The act of walking is to the urban system what the speech act is to language or to statements uttered...It is a spatial acting-out of place'.[22]

While the ideas of Augé and Virilio have been enthusiastically embraced by many contemporary artists working within a site-based context – I am thinking in particular of Graeme Miller and Anna Best – they are nevertheless contradicted by our daily experience of the world.[23] For all the emphasis supposedly placed on speed, many of our everyday activities are characterized by stasis and endless waiting. The cultural theorist Ben Highmore is particularly perceptive about this. Writing in favour of Henri Lefebvre's notion of rhythmanalysis as the methodology best suited to grasp the 'contradictions of urban modernity', Highmore notes:

> I can, for instance, fly from one city to another at speeds that make motorway travel appear ludicrously slow. But my experience and perception of speed is not necessarily determined by this knowledge. Waiting for two or more hours in an airport, to be followed by a seven-hour flight of cramped immobility, air travel might well be experienced as sedentary travel, where time is elongated by the lack of any physicality of movement...For those who submit to the relentlessness of the machine, the experience is often one of slowing-down, time stretching out, a torturous boredom as the line sluggishly and insistently moves; fast enough to stop you doing anything else, slow enough to leave you constantly waiting.[24]

Highmore's Lefebvrian-influenced description of the numbing stasis so characteristic of supermodernity calls for a more nuanced reading of pedestrian performance. From this perspective, pedestrian performance is not so much a return to 'slowness' (the preferred option of Augé and Virilio) as a quest to find a more fluid and mobile mode of interaction with our surroundings, one which is based on a self-generated rhythm. From Highmore's perspective, walking allows the individual to experience the world at a rhythm which digital technology denies with its constant interruptions and breakdowns.[25]

If walking is a revolt against the paradoxical stasis induced by modern communication and transport systems, it is also a reaction against the passivity produced by what the situationist Guy Debord famously called 'the society of the spectacle'. For Debord, spectacularization is not simply to do with the triumph of the image in an aesthetic sense; rather, it concerns the triumph of the image in a total sense – that is to say, the moment when individual consciousness and social relationships have been colonized by representation alone: 'The spectacle is not a collection of images, but a social relation among people, mediated by images'.[26] According to the situationists, wandering or what they called 'drifting' through the city is an antidote to spectacularization. Instead of passively registering the world of images and spectacles, drifting allows the individual to encounter and to imagine the world actively. The drifter or *dériviste* is thus a producer – and not a consumer – of meaning. The cityscape is his/her stage. In keeping with the avant-garde agenda of the situationists, this form of aesthetic re-appropriation is intended to have distinct social and political consequences.[27] Like Henri Lefebvre, their one-time companion and fellow-traveller, the situationists believed that to change space is to change society.[28]

In recent years, Debord's notion of the drift or *dérive* has become increasingly popular with performance makers and theorists, many of whom regard it as a technique for resisting a world dominated by spectacular communication systems: mobile phones, ipods, MP3 players, digital cameras, palm-tops, bluetooth headsets, etc.[29] Where the personal entertainment devices listed above narcissistically cocoon the individual from the public space through which s/he moves, drifting provides the walker with the opportunity for paying attention to his/her surroundings, and, importantly, for meeting fellow citizen-walkers. Rebecca Solnit observes:

> To use a Situationist word, there seems to be a psychogeography of insurrection in which life is lived in public and is about public issues, as manifested by the central ritual of the march, the volubility of strangers and of walls, the throngs in streets and plazas, and the intoxicating atmosphere of potential freedom that means the imagination has already been liberated.[30]

While I have much sympathy with the politics involved in this argument, and think that they are broadly correct, care needs to be taken if we are understand the complex significance behind the recent desire 'to drift'. Too often, it seems that the drift is nostalgically imagined as a way of recovering an authentically human, pre-technological mode of social space.[31] Such a thesis is problematic, for it overlooks how technology unwittingly produces a new demand for pedestrian performance in a manner that contradicts its initial intention.

If we accept as a premise the idea that technology produces different forms of consciousness, then new digital gadgets such as the remote control, the mobile phone and the ipod, which disrupt older, more focused forms of attention, have undoubtedly made us more impatient and greedy for instant communication. We are, as a poet once famously said, 'distracted from distraction by distraction'. Despite the political dangers inherent in such a confused mindset (for instance, the failure to maintain and/or sustain a coherent critique of reality and everyday life), this lack of fixity ought not to be seen in purely negative terms. On the contrary, the distracted and fragmentary consciousness produced by digital technology is, I would claim, one of the prime factors behind the recent interest in pedestrian performance. Contrary to popular opinion, to walk through a landscape does not calm thought or focus the mind; rather, it subjects the mind and body to a plethora of different sensations and perceptions (aural, kinetic, visual). To walk is to be distracted, and to find aesthetic pleasure – perhaps even a kind of transcendence – in that distraction. In other words, the consciousness of the walker is similar to the consciousness of the digital channel hopper or game player; both are dynamic and simultaneous. This leads me to the following conclusion: namely, that the new interest in pedestrian performance, although a reaction against the passivity of spectacularity, is nevertheless produced by the very technological devices that work so hard to sustain the spectacle.

Such an argument has important political consequences – it suggests that all strategies of domination, no matter how pervasive, are ultimately doomed to failure. Like dark stars, they finish by collapsing in on themselves. In terms of cultural politics, this means that the political moment is not to be located in Theodor Adorno and Max Horkheimer's notion of high-brow 'negative aesthetics'.[32] Rather, it implies that the real battle-line, as the avant-garde has always known, is found in popular entertainment forms that are initially designed to reinforce alienation. Because these forms, in my view, eventually implode when spectators get bored of them, they encourage individual users to seek other forms of aesthetic experience. With regard to pedestrian performance, the aesthetic experience sought is the very opposite of the passive and disciplinary experience disseminated by contemporary audio-visual technology.[33]

Whereas mass-media technology strives to enforce what Debord calls 'separation' from one's environment,[34] pedestrian performance attempts to overcome that separation by making us more sensitive to the rhythmic dialogue that occurs between our bodies and the landscapes we walk through. To that extent, technology does not, as many have suggested, disenchant the cosmos per se; paradoxically, it has the potential to re-enchant the world by encouraging the pedestrian performer to discover alternative relationships with landscape based on memory and imagination. In its moment of apparent triumph, then, mass-media technology outwits itself and produces a subject who begins to look beyond the spectacle of technology for different forms of aesthetic pleasure. In doing so, s/he rediscovers the tradition of the marvellous that has been a constant presence in avant-garde thought from Charles Baudelaire and Arthur Rimbaud onwards. Like his/her poetic predecessors, the contemporary walker is seeking ways to re-enchant existence and to find meaning in the world. In an age of impending ecological catastrophe, the enchanted sensibility of the walker is both ethical and political. It points forward to an alternative way of being in, and caring for, the world.

Mourning Walk: Enchantment, Reverie and Healing

Mourning Walk is composed of two separate yet interrelated performances, each of which fulfils a different function. The initial performance (the walk itself) was conceived as a rite of passage, a journey that was intended to have therapeutic consequences; while the second performance – the documentation of the walk – was designed to be performed for an audience. *Mourning Walk* takes de Certeau's notion of 'the long poem of walking' seriously.[35] However, unlike him, I do not see walking as a simple analogy for writing, an equivalent to language. Rather I consider it as a mysterious mode of language production, a bodily rhythm to tease out the strange song of self. I wanted to create an autobiographical text that would fold together memory, reverie and landscape. In retrospect, however, I wonder if the two (the walk and the work) can be so neatly separated? Is not all writing, all art, a response to a loss of some kind, an imaginative way of dealing with lack? And if this is so, then is not writing an enchantment or spell that heals the self by allowing it to recover the past through signs? As I use it, the word recovery has nothing to do with re-experiencing the lost object in its original pristine state; rather, it designates a poetic or an enchanted process in which the subject negotiates the past from the standpoint of the present. In this model, enchantment (poeticization) is dependent upon the impossibility of return, the realization that we are always distanced and already departed.

In *The Poetics of Reverie: Childhood, Language and the Cosmos*, the phenomenologist Gaston Bachelard draws attention to the intimate relationship that exists between reverie and memory. Bachelard is particularly interested in how the poetic image connects with the 'nocturnal' memories of childhood:

> These memories which live by the image and in virtue of the image become, at certain times of our lives...the origin and matter of a complex reverie: the memory dreams, and reverie remembers. When this reverie of remembering becomes the germ of a poetic work, the complex of memory and imagination becomes tightly meshed; it has multiple and reciprocal actions which deceive the sincerity of the poet. More exactly, the happy childhood memories are told with a poet's sincerity. The imagination ceaselessly revives and illustrates the memory.[36]

Importantly for Bachelard, the capacity of reverie to evoke 'the living childhood within us' has healing qualities. By allowing the daydreamer to 'inhabit...the happiness of the world',[37] reverie unites him/her with the effusive, creative principle that, according to him, lies at the heart of the cosmos:

> Suddenly such a dreamer is a *world dreamer*. He opens himself to the world, and the world opens itself to him. One has never seen the world well if he has not dreamed what he was seeing. In a reverie of solitude which increases the solitude of the dreamer, two depths pair off, reverberate in echoes which go from the depths of being of the world to a depth of being of the dreamer...Time is engulfed in the double depth of dreamer and world.[38]

Bachelard's poet, 'the world dreamer', is ostensibly a modern-day Orpheus, a subject who enters the daydream of reverie in order to allow the ghosts of the (human) world and (inhuman) cosmos to speak. In this impossible exchange, this enchanted communication, the subject, Bachelard notes, opens himself to the Other. For me, the transcendence that Bachelard speaks of here has existential effects: it is what allows the subject to affirm loss and to accept death.

In *Mourning Walk*, I was acutely aware of a curious temporal paradox: the further I advanced in real time and space, the more I seemed to lose myself in memory and daydream. There were times, for instance, on the walk, when I had the impression that past and present had entirely collapsed, and that I had magically returned to other landscapes which, for some reason or other, had, until that moment, remained hidden and out of reach. I remembered driving with my Dad in the late afternoon on a gloomy winter solstice thinking of Christmas; swimming in the Bristol Channel under a hot sun; and sheltering from lightning under a tree on the Beach Road, Llantwit Major when my Mum and brother were visiting relatives in Belfast. This autobiographical aspect of walking, its capacity for remembrance, is supported by the comments of the artist and walker Hamish Fulton:

When walking alone, nothing is deflected. A walk has a life of its own ... The flow of influences *should* be from nature to me, not from me to nature. Through art-making I feel a continuity with my childhood and always carry a mental image of the Northumbrian landscape.[39]

Although Fulton recognizes that each walk has 'a life of its own' and thus cannot be known in advance, he also draws attention to a perennial feature of walking: its ability to allow the subject to relive his/her formative experiences of the world. In this way, Fulton confirms the relationship that, I believe, exists between walking and Bachelard's notion of reverie, or what I have called enchantment.

Like enchantment, walking is a synthetic act that combines a series of opposites in a dynamic dialogue: inner/outer, past/present, the poetic/real. Moreover, the point of that dialogue, as in Bachelardian reverie, is to open the subject to him/herself and to the world at large. As I have already mentioned, during the ritualistic phase of *Mourning Walk* I was aware of living more in the past than in the present. However at no time did this immersion in memory result in psychic saturation or disintegration. The natural world – the world of trees and stones – was stubbornly present and insisted on maintaining its autonomy and distance. More to the point, the experience of being in that environment, its assault on my senses, appeared to be the very cause of my enchantment. By encouraging me to dream, the landscape acted as a mnemonic transporting me back to what Bachelard calls 'the solitude of childhood'. This strange spatio-temporal disjunction had a galvanizing effect. I felt a sense of expansion, as if something fragile and hidden was on the point of emerging. To that extent, as I have tentatively hinted at, it does not seem farfetched to claim walking, as an alternative form of psychotherapy, an activity in which enchantment acts as a bridge between past and present, self and cosmos, life and death.

From Autobiography to Autobiology

In her essay 'A Cosmography of Self: The Autobiology of Rachel Rosenthal', Bonnie Marranca argues that Rosenthal avoids the dangers of solipsism that threaten all forms of autobiographical performance by 'accept[ing] ... natural history as part of the history of the world and part of her history'.[40] For Marranca, Rosenthal is not so much concerned with speaking from a particular location or site as with speaking 'tectonically', getting under the surface of things:

> Rosenthal's sense of continental drift has real repercussions in her life, as well as scientific legitimacy. She, Rachel Rosenthal, living at the end of the twentieth century, is part of a process that began about 250 million years ago, when the continents of the earth formed a single mass, called Panagea, which broke up into several continents that have been drifting ever since. As she reads the signs of her life in the earth itself the semiological swells into the seismological. Nothing is what it seems. But now she has a radical understanding of time and space.[41]

According to Marranca, Rosenthal's radically expansive notion of subjectivity articulates an environmental ethics, for it illustrates how identity is necessarily entangled with the destiny of the planet. To be human is to be responsible for, and answerable, to the non-human.

Although I had not read Marranca's essay before making *Mourning Walk*, her argument certainly expresses what I was trying to achieve by including so many different types of map in my own performance (geological, historical, personal, botanical, etc.). As much as the walk allowed me to re-enchant the self, it focused my attention on the landscape that I was in. As I stood on the seam of Jurassic rock that runs through the counties of Rutland and Northamptonshire, it was impossible not to feel part of a seemingly infinite cosmological process, of experiencing what geologists call a sense of 'deep' time. In *Mourning Walk*, as Rachel Rosenthal's work shows, self and environment are umbilically connected. The intimate is always 'extimate', and the personal always planetary. In this context, enchantment is not simply a tool or pretext for poetic purposes alone; rather, it is an attempt to develop an imaginative relationship with the world, a form of 'soft' knowledge that encourages the subject to let things be, to encounter the uncanniness of the cosmos – the very source of the creative imagination.

The Aesthetics and Ethics of Autobiography

Mourning Walk is an autobiographical performance that plays on the difference between absence and presence. To that extent, *Mourning Walk* has more in common with the site-specific practices of artists such as Robert Smithson and Richard Long than with the work of site-specific theatre practitioners such as Mike Pearson (*Bubbling Tom*), Deborah Warner (*The Angel Project*) and Janet Cardiff (*The Missing Voice*). Where Pearson *et al.* are concerned with 'presentness', with performing in the landscape, Smithson is interested in setting up a dialectical negotiation between site and non-site. Smithsonian dialectics are founded on an interplay between presence (the site of the work) and absence (the non-site or gallery where the work is exhibited).

What appeals to me most about this dialectic is the way in which Smithson distinguishes between the act of experiencing the site (the moment of immersion) and the act of producing work from the site (the moment of abstraction). In the essay 'A Sedimentation of the Mind: Earth Projects', he states that, 'the artist who is physically engulfed tries to give evidence of this experience through a limited (mapped) version of the original unbounded state'.[42] The word engulfed is resonant here, for it describes, with accuracy, my physical/existential experience of the site that I performed in – that is, the eighteen miles walked between Market Harborough and Cottesmore on 29 July 2004. There was no way I would have (or could have) produced work from that engulfment. I wanted to share my experience of mourning brought about by the walk, not my experience of mourning *in* the walk. In other words, I was interested in mediation, which, by its very nature, presupposes an economy of lack and loss.

Although they played a major role in determining the shape or structure of *Mourning Walk*, aesthetic concerns were not the sole reason for my reticence. There were important ethical questions to take into account, too. In the West, due to the influence of Christianity and the emphasis placed on confession, ethics have been conventionally associated with transparency, with having nothing to hide. This relationship, however, is complicated in an autobiographical performance context for a number of reasons. First, because performance places a fictional 'frame' around any event, it invariably troubles the status or 'truth' of the situation presented or represented; second, because performance puts the self on display, it necessarily transforms the performer's life into an object of consumption or entertainment; and third, autobiographical performance, while it is very much a solo event, invariably concerns other people. The dilemmas posed by the last point are profound and are succinctly expressed by the following nexus of questions: under what jurisdiction, and in whose name, can we legitimately claim to speak for/ of the other in a public context? This, for me, is where the ethical crux of autobiographical performance lies. As I see it, the issue, then, does not concern fabrication as such (we are, after all, speaking about performance), but, rather, the performer's capacity for respecting the privacy – the singularity – of the other. For obvious reasons, this was particularly pertinent to *Mourning Walk*, since I could not ask my father for permission. Such an ethical position reverses the importance conventionally attached to notions of transparency in the West, for here the emphasis is placed on limits, on purposefully keeping a secret.

My attempt to resolve this ethical problem – to speak about someone while not speaking about them – is ultimately what structured the site/non-site dynamic of *Mourning Walking*. I wanted to perform a ritual for my Dad, something that was intimate and could only apply to us, and, at the same time, to produce an aesthetic object that could be shared with strangers. My response to this duality was to plan the walk that took place on 29 July 2004 as a site-specific ritual and to use the material generated by the walk – the text of *Mourning Walk* – as a non-site-specific performance. To be clear about this: the public side of the piece dealt with emotions and memories generated during the walk, while the private side of the performance referred to a ritual act that I performed at the end of the walk. It is also important to note that I made no attempt to represent my father in an objective light in *Mourning Walk*. In the text, the memories are highly subjective and tell my side of the story. I take full responsibility for them. In this way, I have tried to hide my Dad's 'secret', while basing the text around him. It goes without saying that the ruses of language and the vagaries of memory make any claims to absolute truthfulness suspect. Nevertheless, I have taken the (perhaps) naïve and impossible risk of striving for sincerity. Only the spectator – or in this case, the reader – will know if I have succeeded.

Conclusion

In the first part of this essay, I explored the reasons behind the current interest in pedestrian performance in the UK; in the second part, I reflected on walking as it related to my own autobiographical performance piece *Mourning Walk*. It seems important then, by way of conclusion, to situate *Mourning Walk* within the larger phenomenon of pedestrian performance. Initially, it seems that *Mourning Walk* has little in common with the neo-situationist approach of practitioners such as Lone Twin, Graeme Miller and Wrights & Sites. Whereas they are largely interested in facilitating various forms of urban intervention that seek to establish 'our right to the city',[43] I am concerned with a more intimate and rural-based mode of performance. However, despite these differences, it would be wrong to think that *Mourning Walk* is divorced from contemporary political concerns. As I understand it, enchantment is best understood as a reclamation act, a way of championing a more poetic engagement with our environment – the very thing that the society of the spectacle denies us.

Here, enchantment is not a method for turning away from the world; on the contrary, it seeks to immerse the walker in the strangeness or otherness of the world. This, for me, is where the political potential of enchantment lies – that is to say, in its capacity for making us interested in, and thus responsible for, larger ecological issues. Equally importantly, enchantment, as I have suggested, provides us with existential sustenance. As a response to loss, it allows us to do the work of mourning and to transcend the depressing melancholia that everywhere besets us and from all directions.

Notes

1. Rebecca Solnit, *Wanderlust: A Short History of Walking* (London: Verso, 2001), p. 272.
2. ibid., pp. 268–69.
3. See this book's bibliography for publication details of texts that are not directly quoted.
4. Mike Pearson and Michael Shanks, *Theatre/Archaeology* (London: Routledge, 2001), p. 149.
5. ibid.
6. ibid.
7. ibid.
8. While there is little doubt that women have been spatially disciplined by patriarchy, we ought not to forget that women have also been active in re-appropriating public space for themselves. See, for instance, the role of women in the Paris Commune and, more recently, the mourning rituals performed by the Mothers of the Disappeared in Argentina. The problem with Rendell's thesis is that it positions women in a purely passive context. It also assumes that walking and looking in the city can be reduced to a single purpose: voyeurism. By contrast, I would claim that there are many ways of looking and walking. However, for all that, it is important to listen to Dee Heddon's caution in this volume. Heddon reminds us that women are still more vulnerable to attack than men in their attempts to exist in public space. The solution to this – and I am sure that Heddon would concur – is not to deny men the ability to walk the city, but rather to transform patriarchal attitudes to women so that cities become truly democratic spaces.
9. I'm using performativity according to its generic (Cultural Studies) sense as a process or act that produces meaning and identity, as well as determining and prescribing given forms of behaviour. While performance and performativity are intimately connected, it is important to insist on their differences.
10. It is important to be precise here. The theoretical dimension of *Theatre/Archaeology* concerns walking as a performative activity, not as an element in theatrical performance.
11. See also Keiller's film *Dilapidated Dwelling*, which was commissioned by Channel 4 in 2000 but has never been broadcast.
12. Patrick Keiller, 'Popular Science', in Ann Gallagher (ed.) *Landscape* (London: British Council, 2001), p. 65.
13. ibid., p. 66.
14. The journey undertaken by Robinson and the Narrator in *Robinson in Space* is, for instance, motivated by Robinson's desire to understand how 'the UK [in the absence of any visible export sector] manages to pay for its imports'. See Patrick Keiller, 'A Conversation Between Patrick Wright and Patrick Keiller' in *London* and *Robinson in Space*, pamphlet accompanying *Robinson in Space* (2005), dir. P. Keiller (London: BFI), p. 19.

15. The American critic Stanton B. Garner Jr makes a similar point in his essay on the work of Fiona Templeton and Loading Deck. See Garner, 'Urban Landscapes, Theatrical Encounters: Staging the City', in Una Chaudhuri and Elinor Fuchs (eds) Land/Scape/Theater (Ann Arbor: University of Michigan Press, 2002), pp. 94–118.

16. Iain Sinclair, Edge of the Orison: In the Traces of John Clare's 'Journey Out of Essex' (London: Hamish Hamilton, 2005), p. 79.

17. My definition of avant-garde performance is influenced by Peter Bürger's reading of the avant-garde in his classic text The Theory of the Avant-Garde (1984).

18. Allen Carlson, Aesthetics and the Environment: The Appreciation of Art, Nature and Architecture (London: Routledge, 2000).

19. See also Nöel Carroll, 'On Being Moved by Nature: Between Religion and Natural History', in Salim Kemal and Ivan Gaskell (eds), Landscape, Natural Beauty and the Arts (Cambridge: Cambridge University Press, 1995).

20. The cultural geographer Denis Cosgrove says, for instance, that 'landscape … represents a way in which certain classes of people have signified themselves and their world through their imagined relationship to nature, and through which they have underlined and communicated their social role and that of others with respect to nature'. See Cosgrove, Social Formation and Symbolic Landscape (London: Croon Helm, 1984), p. 15.

21. Marc Augé, Non-Places: A Geography of Supermodernity (London: Verso, 1995), pp. 119–20.

22. Michel de Certeau, 'Walking in the City', in Gary Bridge and Sophie Watson (eds), The Blackwell City Reader (Oxford: Blackwell, 2002), p. 387.

23. See Carl Lavery, 'Walking the Walk: Talking the Talk, Re-imagining the Urban Landscape – An Interview with Graeme Miller', New Theatre Quarterly, 21(2), 2005, pp. 161–65; and Wrights & Sites, An Exeter Mis-Guide (Exeter: Wrights & Sites, 2003).

24. Ben Highmore, Cityscapes (London & New York: Routledge, 2005), pp. 155–57.

25. Dee Heddon offers alternative, more creative readings of stasis in her texts in this volume.

26. Guy Debord, The Society of the Spectacle (Detroit: Black and Red, 1983), p. 2.

27. The avant-garde agenda of the situationists is different from that of its Dada and Surrealist predecessors. Where Dadaism wanted to abolish art in politics, and Surrealism to abolish politics in art, situationism strove to find a properly dialectic solution to this dichotomy.

28. For a good account of Lefebvre's influence on situationism, see Kristin Ross, 'Lefebvre on the situationists: An Interview with Kristin Ross', October, 79, 1997, pp. 68–83.

29. Most readings that explore the influence of situationism on contemporary theatre practice tend to downplay the role of derive, preferring instead to focus on the notion of the constructed situation. An important exception to this, and one which starts to trace the relationship between situationism and site-specific performance, is found in Branislav Jakovljevic, 'The Space Specific Theatre: Skewed Visions' The City Itself', The Drama Review, 49(3), 2005, pp. 96–106.

30. Solnit, Wanderlust, p. 230.

31. See, for instance, Solnit (2001) and Lippard (1997).

32. Adorno and Horkheimer remark in Dialectic of Enlightenment (London: Verso, 1997):

Serious art has been withheld from those for whom the hardship and oppression of life make a mockery of seriousness, and who must be glad if they can use time not spent at the production line just to keep going. Light art has been the shadow of autonomous art. It is the social bad conscience of serious art. The truth which the later necessarily lacked because of its social premises gives the other the semblance of legitimacy. The division is itself the truth: it does at least express the negativity of the culture which the different spheres constitute. (p. 135)

33. I am also aware that other contemporary practices such as 'flash-mobbing' and 'mobile-clubbing' use digital technology for transgressive ends.

34. Debord, *The Society of the Spectacle*, p. 3.

35. Michel de Certeau, *The Practice of Everyday Life* (Berkeley: University of California Press, 1984), p. 389.

36. Gaston Bachelard, *The Poetics of Reverie: Childhood, Language and the Cosmos* (Boston: Beacon Press, 1991), p. 20.

37. ibid., p. 22.

38. ibid., p. 173.

39. Hamish Fulton, in Jeffrey Kastner (ed.); survey Brian Wallis, *Land and Environmental Art* (London: Phaidon Press, 1998), p. 242.

40. Bonnie Marranca, *Ecologies of Theatre: Essays at the Century Turning* (Baltimore: John Hopkins, 1995), p. 59.

41. ibid., p. 67.

42. Robert Smithson, *Robert Smithson: The Collected Writings* (Berkeley: University of California Press, 1996), p. 104.

43. Henri Lefebvre, *Writings on Cities* (Oxford: Blackwell, 2003), p. 158.

PART 2: PHIL SMITH

THE CRAB WALKS

by Phil Smith

First performance: 11 a.m., 12 July 2004 at beach hut number 3, Coryton Cove, Dawlish. Then 26 subsequent performances there and at beach hut R3, the Point, Teignmouth.

Performer: Phil Smith
Outside eye: Anjali Jay
Map designer: Tony Weaver
Sound artist for CD walk *A Dawlish Warren Low Tide Walk*: Tom Davies
Loan of beach hut: Sean Brogan
Thanks to: Richard Baker and Bob McHardy at the Pirates' Chest
Practical support: Julie Owen, Doff Pollard, Celia Hadow, Mari Sved, Andrea Ayres
Funding and support: Arts Council England, Teignbridge District Council.

Publicity image for *The Crab Walks*. Photo: Julie Owen. Image adjustment: Mari Sved.

The Crab Walks

[*Performed in a beach hut. Objects in this space include: a small octagonal carved table and a small brown pouffe; OS map of the area; the book Cock'ood and the Warren: An Historical View, edited by Skip Skerrett and Nigel Stoneman; pack of modelling clay; rucksack.*

Once audience are settled and greeted, I move into a slipping and sliding walk – elide into the performance from pre-show chat with the audience.]

1: The Gulls Attack

I'm walking down the edge of the River Teign ... the signs say this is the Templer Way, but I'm not convinced this is anything ... 'Have we lost the path?' [*Bend down as if picking up crab shell.*] We're finding all these empty crab shells – lots of them, everywhere. I say to Anjali: 'They've been eaten very efficiently by something! Look, there's just a little hole behind the legs. I reckon they've been hollowed out by herring gulls.'

[*Cry like a herring gull.*]

I thought those herring gulls were going to hollow me out. Have you ever seen the Alfred Hitchcock film *The Birds*? There's a great shot in it: it's from right up above, right up with the gulls, and they're looking down on this burning gas station in America. It's an image I have in my head for how I can see things when I'm walking. It's a great film – all about birds turning on people – of course, Daphne Du Maurier wrote the story about somewhere just down the coast from here ... for a long time on my walks I felt that the gulls were looking down on me like they looked down on that gas station.

This trouble with herring gulls all started when I was coming up the steps by the Old Quay docks in Teignmouth ... next to Number 1 Warehouse. I did see the gulls on the roof at the top, but I thought – 'well...' – the next moment the gulls are screaming and gathering. I run into the little square at the top.

[*Me, bending, running and hiding in doorway, back against the back of the hut, peering out.*]

It's a real hub of a place. I'm hiding in a doorway. And it makes me wait and look at where I am. There are little commercial premises that aren't properly advertised, but mysterious ... I'm having to really look at this now ... I can see on the other side of the square this edifice of a building, with an indoor bowls club over a funeral parlour – I imagine a green, baize heaven ... was a fish store, storing 'toe rag' – dried cod salted in Newfoundland with salt from the Haldon Hills above Teignmouth and shipped back smelling of socks – after that it was a prison and before that a lot of it was a volcano. There's a sailing boat I can dimly see through frosted glass ...

[*Cry of gulls. I'm ducking.*]

...the gulls are going mad now and history is circling above my head and there must be fifty or so of them hovering about fifteen feet off the ground. I take out my notebook to make a sketch of the unusual pattern on the house at the bottom of Willow Street. I walk out...

[*Angry gull noises. Me, running. Ducking and diving.*]

I take flight across a metal bridge, over the railway – to the right a beautiful, bare, little, symmetrical world of washing lines – I'm noticing these places really vividly – to the left a bleak, small world of fenced in nothingness, hacked off chunks of a shrub have swallowed bits of the wire.

The gulls are dropping away now, but there are still one or two swooping and hovering low. I'm trying to keep calm, making notes as I go!! I don't forget those little places I fled through... [*Breathless.*] I'm walking steadily now, heart pumping, sailors pass by speaking in French [*a snatch of conversation in French*], every time I look up I see a gull on a roof...even The Street With No Name is The Street With A Gull...I'm walking over the ballast from foreign ships used for the foundations of the town centre, the volcanic lava in the undertakers is flowing. Everything is originally from somewhere else.

2: Why the Walk

I shouldn't really be telling you about *running*. This is supposed to be about a special kind of *walking* I did...I think I ought to tell you what that walk was all about, before we get any further down the path...

You see, I was walking from Dawlish Warren to Paignton...but not like the other walkers I'd meet along my way. I wasn't that interested in getting to a particular destination, I wasn't there for my health – though it didn't do me any harm...I was taking my time...doing it in bits...going home and starting again...beginning in the middle...I was heading off the path all the time...I was looking for something, I was looking for connections...because this coast is where I used to come for my special holidays, you see. My Nan and Pop would take me out of school for a couple of days – not supposed to do that really, are you? – and they'd bring me down here to stay off-season in a guest-house at Paignton and we'd explore up and down the coast. I was about ten; we'd tell my sister I was going to train with the Territorial Army so she wouldn't be jealous. And for a couple of days I'd live in this off-season heaven. My Nan and Pop would make me feel like all the places that weren't shut were open specially for me. I think that's why I love those old TV programmes like *The Avengers*, when everyone in the world but the heroes fall asleep and there's free shopping everywhere.

And this walk was about finding that precious feeling again. When this seaside was that magical playground for me.

I'm feeling rather disorientated by now. I see... [*Pick up table*] the unusual shape of the church of St James the Less...and I cross the main road to have a look. [*Looking out in front.*] A notice on the church said I was outside the visiting times, but the door is open. I believe in wandering into places. The world's too full of security guards. I go in.

[*Put the table down before audience.*]

'1268–1968 Pride In the Past, Praise For the Present, Faith in The Future'. 1968: the year that Donald Crowhurst sailed the Teignmouth Electron past the Ness and out into open waters.

This octagonal shaped church is one of only two in England. It's very strange that they should change it from the shape of the cross – perhaps there's a link to the Dome of the Rock in Jerusalem ... or to Christopher Wren's St Pauls ... some people think there's a secret geometry passed down by masons and architects in the shapes of buildings, secrets hidden in the very arrangements of the stones: the octagon is the shape that brings the divine and the earthly together – the circle is divine, the square is earthly, together they make an octagon.

[*Draw circle with one hand and square with the other. Then push the invisible shapes together. Move the table back to its starting position.*]

We'd always stay in the same guest-house in Paignton – run by Jeff and Joy who were friends of my Nan and Pop – and the next door guest-house was run by the mother of either Jeff or Joy. I forget which. Opposite was a big hotel I remember as sandy red and magical, like a fairy castle ... in fact, it's not red, it's called 'red' ... the Redcliffe Hotel. It's a wormhole to India, its different parts based on famous Indian buildings – and that's why Anjali was with me, because I wanted to travel not just back and forward across time, but also across a little of the sensibility of this planet.

[*Walking again, slipping.*]

3: Still Slipping and Sliding
So there I was ... on those slippery rocks, worrying a little bit for Anjali – 'Are you ok?' Anjali's an Indian-born actress, just come from touring to New York with the Royal Shakespeare Company's production of *Midnight's Children*. 'I'm sorry about this ... be careful of your footing ...' Anjali was a classical dancer until she injured her back. I don't want her doing any more damage ... 'Phew, this is hard work. This is like that very hot day I told you about – when I was struggling up Upper Woodbury Road – on the other side of the river? ... I was telling you about that strange area up there on the top of Little Haldon, I'll take you up there, later ...' And as I'm telling Anjali, I'm seeing again the burned-out shell of an old people's home on my left – like a huge version of one of these empty crab shells. I sneak around in its gardens a little ... and a voice shouted 'Phil!!' – [*Look around.*] 'Phil!!' – but it must have been for another 'Phil'. Maybe the one I was becoming.

I'd got lost coming out of Teignmouth. [*Pointing.*] A helpful woman said 'excuse me for pointing', as if the landscape might be offended.

I pass an electricity substation, humming conspiratorially – like monks. My friend Tom is with me this time – he's come to make sound recordings, but he can't pick up the hum on his machine. The place is like a ghostly temple ruin. Crumbling concrete pillars and invisible energy. Electricity is so scary, it's its own security. Most of us walk past those things, we probably think they're ugly ... and we definitely think the pylons are ... do you know where that word 'pylon' comes from? Pylons are the doors between one room and the next in the Egyptian afterlife, a little bigger at the bottom than the top. When you begin to see pylons and substations like that – carrying the energy we would once have called life, or soul, or ka, or spirit – you begin to see the beauty, because they look outside how we are inside. The brain is electrical. I like to think there are thoughts running down those wires [*Look up*] – like souls through the passageways of the dead.

[*Steady myself with hand on the back wall.*]

But now, I'm more worried about the slippery riverbed. [*Looks ahead.*] 'It's not far to the estuary!'

But I say to Anjali that *she's* got to guide us to the Ness – by whatever route she wants, even though she doesn't have a map and she doesn't know where she is. This is a way you can find new places, unexpected places, allow yourself to be led by someone who doesn't know where they are going. At Anjali's command, we cut inland through deserted lanes, past a cricket pitch in the middle of nowhere, and then through a medieval village where invisible people are mending an old barn ...

[*Knock on table with a coin to imitate sound of hammering.*]

... we eat wonderful food at the Wild Goose pub, [*Showing delight!*] sitting in its garden, with the church, and the sheep in the field, and beautiful cranky shed-like keeling lean-tos. While I'm eating my faggots, Anjali tells me that the day has taken her back to her childhood in Bangalore, reading Famous Five adventures ...

But the more I'd walked the less I could remember. Everywhere I went I seemed to see for the first time. And yet I really wanted to get back to those feelings I'd had. I thought maybe they were tucked in the sands of one of the little beaches somewhere ... or under some weed in a rock pool. When my Pop died my Nan said: 'he loved you, you know' – and that isn't a word generally overused in our family. I remember that feeling of returning through the mist to Paignton Harbour – just me and Pop and the fisherman – feeling safe in the mist, wrapped up warm in my old rust jumper. My Nan's pancakes in the shapes of any animals I wanted ... elephants, octopuses, and then the sugar and lemon ... those were the feelings I wanted to get back ... the shapes and sugar and lemon of being a kid, the stick of rock and the sea-smelling crabs in a bucket. My Nan was a glass blower, my Pop was a pattern-maker.

4: Dawlish Warren

[*Taking OS map and opening at the Dawlish Warren part.*]

I'd started my search at Dawlish Warren station on the 16th of June 2003. When I got off the train at Dawlish Warren, I found that the first place I'd intended to visit – the old wooden station house – had been burned down the day before. There was a handwritten sign: 'Arson. 5 am at the Old Station'. My first thought was, 'Bloody kids – this wouldn't have happened in the past' and I carried on thinking that until I found *this* picture in this book about Cock'ood and Dawlish Warren... there it is again, the station house on Dawlish Warren burning down sometime in the 1920s and the writer's just the same as me... suspecting the young boys in the picture of having something to do with it... What did that say about me? What had I become? Especially when I remembered not being entirely unconnected to setting fire to the back of our shops.

I didn't go straight to the beach or to the Warren. I walked past the mis-engraved bench for Walter Erich Witt 'with treasured mememories – here he found peace and tranquillity'.

[*As if I'm seeing all this.*]

I go up the hill, past the Langstone Cliff hotel... turn right down the lane past Golden Sands Holiday Park and a quarter mile further down there's this doorway suspended four feet up the side of the bank. An hour later I find myself on the other side of the hovering gateway, inside the Lady's Mile Holiday Park. I sit down among the fairy rings – there's a great bowling view to big white buildings. It says 'hospital' on the map, but they look like the kind of buildings where sinister things happen in old Quatermass movies. There's a big house up there too – but I've never been there... perhaps its connected to the weirdness up on the top of Little Haldon... all I know is that it's called Mamhead House – because it's built on a hill shaped like a woman's breast.

Two weeks later Tom, the sound man, and me, are walking back from here. 'What is this place, Tom? This is a strange place. No name. [*Reads.*] "No unauthorized chemicals permitted on this site."'

[*Look about. Acting out this dialogue.*] 'It's a big place. Kind of... somewhere out of mid-west nowhere bad movie USA.'

'Uhuh. Jeepers Creepers 2.'

'It's new.'

'Well, it's already haunted.'

It looks unmanned. Automatic...

[*Change of tone.*]

But two eyes are watching us all the time. They come over.

'What's happening? What's the crack?' he says, pretending to be friendly, but he's aggressive, interrogating. Maybe he thinks we're terrorists... or maybe he's pretending to think we're terrorists... so we can be terrorized by the suggestion that we are...

We're acting out a little microcosm of the world...

'Which way are you walking next?' Trouble is, I never know where this walking will take me.

[*Sit down.*]

I suggest you have a drink on the veranda at the Langstone Cliff Hotel. There's a wonderful view of Ladrum Bay over the water. But when I look over there I see something I could never have seen. My Dad in his RAF jet diverting off course to fly over the beach there, to waggle its wings for my Mum and my Nan and Pop sunning themselves below, by the great red towers of sandstone.

A careful lady is seated at the next table: 'It's a lovely place, isn't?' she says to me.

[*I nod. Smile. Then take in the view. Pause.*]

And the land looks back at us.

[*Then, light and conversational:*] On the way down to the sea, the posters say: 'medieval jousting – as seen on TV'. I didn't know TV was so old.

[*Take out lots of Giggles Fun Shop props – wind-up clockwork toy penis, etc. – from rucksack and arranging on the table.*]

Giggles Fun Shop is like an erotic temple... there are regiments of phallic ice cube makers and chorus lines of mechanical dancing pussies... celebrations of the male and the female. Like the Hindu linga and yoni, the male and female forms in nature. If you look for them they're everywhere: the Cow's Hole just here in Boat Cove is a yoni; there are lingum shaped gateposts on the steps right next to us. Shapes rise up. Religions form by accident. These shapes are more profound than sexual – and the same for the novelties in Giggles Fun Shop. They are part of a pattern – the god Brahma tried to find the top of it, the god Vishnu tried to find the bottom of it – neither succeeded – so the pattern goes looping round the world. The curved space of the universe.[1]

I walk under the Creep and to the end of the Warren.

[Back to the 'stage left' wall. Looking inwards.]

It's hard to believe that in that bleak and empty place – where Christmas trees are buried under the sand to keep it from washing away – [Taking in the sight of the houses.] – just 70 years ago, a community lived in houses built on sand. [Follow with eyes the trajectory of a tennis ball, looping right to left.] But all I could sense of them was the cry of a tennis player on the wind...'out!' [Register the ball's impact with nod of the head]...and the ringing of a bell for tea in the rustling and grumbling of the waves, getting nearer and nearer until they're running through the house...[Jump up onto pouffe]...sweeping up the carpets...gurgling round the bath...houses rise up around me...and fall down...ghosts run up flags and flee from the raging tide...

'For when the tide rises it oft seems to say,

Friend Warren, you'd better get out of my way'.[2]

[Break point – time to take a sip of water. Step down from pouffe.]

5: Dawlish
Next morning I set off to walk to Dawlish, along the front. [Climb on pouffe.] I climbed up on the sea wall, and when I turned round to take a photograph there's a policeman striding up the wall after me. Below me to seaward there are three Christmas trees lodged in the rocks. It's not yet 9 a.m. He says: 'We're looking for a man – 47...' I was 47. '...grey hair...' It's me! What's happened?! 'Slim build.' Phew.

The Langstone Cliff Hotel appeared up on my right, nestled in a dip, snug in its modern skeleton, like a hermit crab.

A sign reads: 'Railtrack plc hereby give notice that this way is not dedicated to the public' – like the railway then.

[Jump down from pouffe straight into sitting position.]

'Look there it is, Pop – Dawlish!!' [As a young me.]

'How's it going?' She looks in my sketchbook. 'Beautiful.' [This as my Nan.]

There's a sign beside the railway line – of a leaf.

[Stand up.]

Before I get to the front at Dawlish I cut inland. I find a footpath called Commons Lane, crumpled metal buckets in its earthen wall. I climb a stile into a field...

Policeman approaching, sea wall at Dawlish Warren. Photo: Phil Smith.

[*Climb over pouffe.*]

...you get a sort of feeling when you are about to find somewhere special. It's to do with the shapes of a place. It's like you are sliding down into a basin of attraction. [*Slide!*] Even if you're walking uphill there's no effort in the walking. [*'Floating' uphill.*] Because you're walking a different kind of physics. Albert Einstein discovered that gravity – the thing that holds us onto the earth – [*Pushing down on the table*] – also pulls everything else – [*Pulling at the walls of the space*] – so much in fact that space is a series of bends and curves. [*Curving and bending my body.*] And there's a kind of gravity at work here, pulling you towards these special places...

[*Climbing over pouffe.*]

I climb another stile and I'm in it. [*Into hovering eagle posture – arms out like wings with the occasional beat. Eyes observing the land below. Manic pace.*] Beneath me is the inland part of Dawlish, church mysteriously stuck on its edge, holding back the town from rolling grounds with lollipop shaped trees: a selfish giant's garden. All around me, in the edge of the grass are old tree stumps... they seem very old... some meeting place of the ancients. One looks like that mountain Richard Dreyfuss is irrationally drawn to for the alien landing in *Close Encounters of the Third Kind* – seeing its shape everywhere – in pillows, in piles of mash potato. [*Flap wings hard up behind my back.*] I wonder if that church is a St Michael's? It should be! There's something of angels and aliens about this place! The great body of air that hangs above the town, it should be flown by silver craft, curving like hunting mackerel! Under circling birds of prey, Christmas trees are being grown! I imagine them buried under sand! The homes opposite are like thousands of eyes. Argus the many-eyed giant lounging on the hill! This is the place to see it all.

[*Falling, stumbling motion.*]

I fall down a tunnel of small trees! A beached whale skeleton of a huge glassless greenhouse rises up, majestic, pathetic, full of weeds! [*Look up. Then to stage left.*] Then an even bigger hangar-like one, this time glazed, but empty.

[*Hushed.*] I stand in the doorway, wondering if I walk in whether all the roof will fall like melting ice... I've walked through glass once... it was like the inside of my eyes cracked... I stand on the threshold – toppling into the expanse of sunlit space – the emptiness is tangible, syrupy.

'MOTHER, soft and warm, your love enfolds me like petals on a soft red rose.'

[*Reading notice in front of me.*] 'Visitors always welcome' – the church is locked. [*Laugh.*]

[*Squatting down and reading as if off the table as gravestone.*] 'Waiting for redemption here rests the body of Ebenezer Pardon.'

Under a stone pylon.

[*Then, straight to audience, hushed.*] I'm in the graveyard of St Gregory the Great's – the church I'd hoped was a St Michael's and All Angels – an old site of the worship of Mercury ... Later I discovered that for years the church *was* called St Michael's – by 'mistake'! Until someone checked the records and changed it ... but the people KNEW!!

[*Sit on the pouffe.*]

Grandad Smith always sat on the beach in a full three-piece suit and trilby. He was an RSM in the British Army in India. Because of him we had curry at home long before anybody ever went 'out for an Indian'. My dad looked down on people who ate Vesta curries. We had real ones made with Venkat Curry Powder – and a carving of Ganesh – the elephant-headed god, the remover of obstacles – my Dad brought back from Calcutta in the 1970s. We had brass vases and things with swirling plant decorations that Grandad Smith had brought back. And an eight-sided table that looked like the church in Teignmouth. This is it.

6: To Teignmouth

Next day I set off for Teignmouth. I get to Smuggler's Lane and down on the sea wall I can see the Parson and the Clerk off Holcombe. I climb down to the beach and walk a winding path defined by the in and out of the waves.

One day when the Vicar of Dawlish and his Clerk had finished collecting tithes in Teignmouth they set off back home by the cliff path ... when to their surprise ... sometimes there's mist in the story and they get lost despite their familiarity with the route ... when to their surprise they saw a house they'd never seen before – brightly lit and ringing with the sounds of merry-making – and at its door stood the host, beckoning them to join the party. The weather was cold and they were pleased to accept the offer of hospitality and imbibed freely of the drinks they were given. When it came time to go the Parson, disorientated by mist and drink, inquired from his host which way they should take. 'I must have a guide even if it be the Devil himself!' he joked. The host smiled and said he would be their guide. He led them to a road that was unfamiliar to both the Parson and Clerk. Warmed by the wine, though, they set off at speed until they found themselves – suddenly – up to their boot tops in water. A demonic shriek of laughter rang out and a great wave covered the clerics and dragged them out to sea.

The crazy house had vanished –
The breakers surged and ran;
And to the flanks of their horses
Clung master and clung man.

Prone on the rocks next morning
They stretched there, stiff and stark;
On one rock lay the parson,
On one rock lay the clerk.

Beaten and torn and mangled,
They clung with dead-cold hands,
While their horses wandered harmless
On shining Dawlish sands.[3]

And next day two stacks of sandstone stood in the waves where the bodies had disappeared. But...if they drowned, who knew about that shriek of laughter? Who first told the story? It mentions no witnesses. And the Parson and the Clerk were dead.

While you're walking look out for buildings that fade in and out of existence.

[*Jump up, mime towelling water from hair and eyes.*]

At Teignmouth, I swam at the Lido, where an attendant was alternately luring and hosing down the herring gulls. Great – he's going to start a war between humans and gulls!

Cutting sharply inland across one of the bridges over the railway I'm immediately in the badlands – DOGS RUNNING FREE DO NOT ENTER – the tatters of a necktie pinned to metal gates – what is this?

The smell of money – I'm just beyond the Penny Falls – I'm on the pier...there's a pagan machine: 'Hold HAND down firmly on the SENSOR PLATE until your FORTUNE CARD is delivered.' I put my hand on the plate and drop in my small coin: waves of tiny metal stumps massage my palm.

'YOUR Hand denotes a very fine temperamental nature, but you have great ability, especially in Business matters. You will discover easy methods of making money...' At different times Tom and Anjali also have their palms mechanically read. Our FORTUNE CARDS have one thing in common: all three of us will succeed in business.

In 1966 Norman Wisdom made a movie called *Press For Time* in the town. There's a chase sequence when Norman races after a bicyclist on a commandeered double-decker bus. When the film was shown locally it bewildered the audience with its geographical leaps. [*Pointing out with hand.*] At one point Norman alights at the station and emerges from it at the top of the railway bridge walking back towards the station itself. As if he were caught in a loop. [*Making loop gesture with hand.*]

I saw a priest – with a large young woman on his arm – I was sure he was a counterfeit – his dog collar didn't fit him and when I watched him he stared back aggressively...

[*Turning to see:*] 'Live Eels,' says a big sign by the ferry.

'Do you mind if I ask what your interest is?' someone said to me.

'SUPAWASH. We do do duvets.'

That night I catch the train home and there are men digging around the edge of the burned rectangle at Dawlish Warren Station – as if they've lost something, as if they're regretting levelling the ruin so quickly.

7: The Strange Places on the Top

[*Take modelling clay from rucksack bag. Hand out pieces of modelling clay.*]

Anjali and me caught a taxi from Dawlish Station up to Ashcombe, where the church is named after the beheaded saint, Nectan.

A good thing to do if you're out walking is to find a stone that looks a little like your head or pick up a piece of clay and make a little model of your head with it – carry it with you – in your hand, in your pocket – to remind you to look at things from different points of view.

[*Walking.*]

BEWARE PARTRIDGE AND CHICKS BEWARE!! What does it mean? Do not disturb the delicate young birds or expect a violent parent to peck you to pieces?

Ashcombe Tower, a private residence that houses Hitler's personal telephone.

The trees close over our heads. I can see from the map that we are walking between ancient graves.

We emerge over a deep valley of patchwork greens: this is the Tolkien bathing of England.

The remnants of the old Aerodrome Club torched by Hell's Angels in the 1970s.

Oswald Moseley, the British Nazi, landed here, fleeing the rocks Plymouth people had thrown at his plane...

In 1931, Lady Florrie Westenra set out in a DH80A Puss Moth, to find her husband, lost on his yacht...

Routing via Farnborough, the Rhone Valley and Montelimar, Lady Florrie found the Honourable Richard in port on the Riviera.

My Nan had chocolates called Montelimar.

[*Stop walking here.*]

No one went to save Donald Crowhurst. No one knew he was in trouble.

The countryside is riddled with these spirit possessions, these old lines, these wild hunts...

But Lidwell Chapel...ah.

[*Hands parallel in snaking motion.*] I walked a path of flints. [*Rubbing fingers with thumbs.*] Even on a wet day it speaks of dryness and bones. [*Precisely lift up rock with left hand.*] The rock exposed is just under the skin all the way along the tops of these Little Haldon Hills. [*Make voluptuous curve with the left hand.*] The path becomes more and more loaded with dread and apprehension. [*Both hands pressing down.*] A gulf opens up on the left – [*Gesture to the left*] – a parade of trees on the right. [*Gesture to the right. Then palms together and hands – in this shape – pushed towards the audience.*] And, in between, the flints point us into a field of long trouser-soaking grass. [*Interweave fingers, then rotate hands so fingers are on the top, waggling fingers slightly.*] The ruts in the ploughed field are nibbling for a turned ankle. [*Hands out as if to steady myself.*] You stumble all the time with ruins in the corner of your eye. [*Hands in front, palms to chest, then open out like gates and then drop hands to side.*] A couple of iron gates and you are in the chapel of the Mad Monk. In the very floor of what was consecrated ground, the well is still there – like the location for a Japanese horror film – [*As if taking a handful of water from the well*] – down there his victims were stuffed and from there their bones were recovered.

A single wall of the chapel stands, like a hungry one-eyed monster. The Monk would lure women here, rob them and throw their bodies down the well. Or he would disguise himself as a traveller and rob the wealthy. Or he was a child-murderer from another place. Or a rapist from Gidley. Or he was a clerk whose ideas were unorthodox, who defamed the Bishop and was declared a 'satellite of Satan'. Or was thrown down his own well by a devout sailor who raising his eyes to heaven saw the monk's shadow, knife in hand, on the chapel wall – [*I mime the shadow, facing the audience, fingers flickering for the gulls' wings*] – flickering like gulls across a pavement. [*Drop hand to side.*] Or he is a jumbled memory of the violence to the chapel itself – by men of puritan religion who hated the voluptuous curve of an image. [*Making curved S with hand. Then, distorting my own voice and body.*] History stretches and distorts him like some kind of monster: a patchwork, catch-all evil. The place is pulled and bent in the same way. In 1980 a photograph taken of the ruins, when developed, revealed a complete chapel. The photograph has since disappeared.

The Parson and the Clerk is a story. And yet it has left two great piles of sandstone. The Mad Monk is a piece of uncertain history – and yet his stones are ruined, almost disappeared. It was this mixture of stones and stories that I was walking.

After one foray up on the top there I was soon eating scallops – very good ones – at the Ness House Hotel – the waters sweeping down the Teign outside, the same waters that swept Crowhurst out into open seas.

Recording textures at the Mad Monk's chapel on a group drift of the Haldon Hills.

Donald Crowhurst was born in India in 1932. 'To the extent that he was religious, his religion was scientific precision.'[4] His manifesto was a computer program. But all this logic was struggling with another part of him – seeking Black Magic powers.

[*Speaking as circumambulating the table.*] He wanted to circumnavigate the world – in a yacht, single-handed – just as a devout Hindu circumambulates the image of a god.

And yet ... under-prepared – he had only gone a short way before he realized he would never be able to get all the way round ... and the logical, empirical, train-timetable Englishman in him was in combat with the seeker in him, the part that led him to take Albert Einstein's book on 'Relativity' – along with lots of curry.

His tragedy is that the parts were not connected to the whole. Wires ran from all sorts of gadgets and devices all over the Teignmouth Electron, leading to a hole where they ran down under Crowhurst's seat. When the boat was found – and the seat was lifted – [*Lifting the pouffe*] – the wires were found to end only in a tangle. Crowhurst had never had time to build the computer supposed to control it all.

For a moment, not long before the end, he seems to achieve something – seeing the abstract shapes of relativity in the waves around him – but then he cuts his line with the material world. In his log he writes, 'It is finished – It is finished. IT IS THE MERCY'.

Because of him, we can all walk the journey that he pioneered for us – but without the mortal risks. Rather than the world, we can walk around an icon; it might be a building like the Redcliffe Hotel, it might be a rock on the beach, it might be the Haldon Hills or a burned out old people's home ...

[*Circumambulate the table.*]

8: To Paignton
I walked for a day from the Ness until I came to Kent's Cavern in Babbacombe ...

In the Cavern the guide takes the cast of a Neanderthal skull ... big eyes and small brains ... and compares it with the head of one of our party. Yet, we should be careful: but for certain climate changes it might have been a Neanderthal guide showing Neanderthal tourists the skull of a Human ... and laughing at its small eyes and big clumsy brain.

I reach the Strand where, at number 13 a dead child was once delivered by post.

On the beach by the castellated Livermead Cliff Hotel, Phoenician traders landed, taking tin from Dartmoor and leaving behind the recipe for Clotted Cream. Maybe.

Sometimes I am walking like that eccentric of Dawlish they called the Walking Wardrobe. I'm putting costume over costume over costume. [*Miming putting on costume over costume.*]

Family photograph, holidaying in Paignton, circa 1966. Redcliffe Hotel in the background. Phil Smith seated at the back of the boat. Photo: Bernard Smith.

Feeling that at any moment I might reach through the fur coats inside and feel my way back to Narnia. Or Nan.

On the furthest Paignton beach Monty Python filmed a cupboard with ferocious teeth that came out of the sea and chased Carol Cleveland up the sands, the spines of cactus plants removing her clothes one by one by one as she ran – [*Miming the removal of the clothes*] – the Walking Wardrobe in reverse.

But I didn't find my memories. Misty mackerel fishing in my rust red jumper. Other than the occasional dusty window display, that world has gone. I did find it again – at a Hungarian holiday resort. But not here.

I had found something bigger... I'd found all these layers – the gulls, the giant's eyes, the shifting sands of ghost houses, the Christmas trees under the Marram grass, the Neanderthal under Babbacombe.

But my memory is like The Redcliffe Hotel now: a lot of it is missing – the minarets have gone – the echoes from the Qutb Minar Mosque almost silenced.

Nan and Pop weren't missing. I felt the presence of their love. The adventure, the safety, the warmth inside the cold out on a misty, shaky sea. But I couldn't find it HERE anymore.[5]

So, with Anjali, I went to knock on the door of the guest-house where we used to go and stay. One last try for memory.

I wasn't going to call, but there was no lunch available at the Redcliffe Hotel – and, as we came out, I thought – why not? I'd been putting this off. Why the hell? So Anjali and me made our way over to the guest-house where I'd had those happy childhood times...

[Me *ringing on doorbell. I physicalize myself and the hotel owner.*]

'um...this is a bit of an odd request...'

'I'm VERY busy...'

'oh...'

'wait there...two minutes...'

And he goes and we stand there. I think of Nan and Pop and coming here and I start to feel the presence of the place and I feel some tears coming that I fight back. I can't reconcile the happiness of the memories and the abruptness of this. I can't put together the security I know I once felt here and now this hovering on the doorstep, excluded. He comes back.

'Right. I'm very busy...'

'Um, well my name's Phil Smith and I'm a writer and I'm working on an autobiography...'

He reacts, but I plough on.

'...and I came here a lot when I was young and I wondered if we could quickly have a look round...'

He shakes his head.

'No. You've chosen the busiest time – I've got 8 to 10 hours of work ahead of me...'

Anjali and me are going: 'oh, right...right...oh, well...' and retreating down the drive. Perhaps he thinks I'm another John Cleese – come to trash Torbay hotel owners – but why is he acting like Basil Fawlty?

My head is chopped off – like the decapitated ghosts of Old Lime Avenue – but an elephant head grows in the place of mine. I remember. I realize now this has never been an autobiographical walk. I've been walking for other people. The memories I have...are not mine. They're not just the past – not just Nan and Pop and Jeff and Joy. Although I'll always love my Nan and Pop and remember them and wish I'd loved them more and better when they were alive and wished I hadn't left my Pop with sharp words the last time I saw him alive. No – this walk through nostalgia is a walk into the future, a pioneering wander through the familiar, only to find everything changed and full of endless wonder. But the wonder looks back at you, looks into you, and you look back at it.

A confectionary fish disappearing up a drainpipe.

A four-foot-high bottle of milk on a gatepost.

The musical notes on a choirmaster's gravestone.

Inside every holiday, there's another holiday to be had.

I'm on the outskirts of Paignton, alone, picking out an overgrown path, climbing up hidden steps made of railway sleepers, and I enter a world where I can hear no cars, I can hear no planes. Only insects and water and birdcalls and a rippling sea of greens and yellows. I disappear into the pattern of a butterfly. I begin to feel all the experiences of my walking becoming a pattern, a map, something I can fold up and put in my inside pocket. [*Touches heart.*] I see where all the different routes connect up. Donald Crowhurst and those rowing boats full of flowers in Shaldon. Herring gulls and electrons. If only I could leap like them and not fear where I might end up.

[*Then leap up, almost a showbiz pose.*]

Ganesh is the god of overcoming obstacles!!

I have to have one last go! [*Indicating with hands the position of the guest-house.*] Next door to the guest-house where we always stayed there is another. It had been owned by either Jeff or Joy's mother and we would sometimes go round there in the evening ... maybe there I could remember something.

[*I ring on the doorbell.*]

A woman answers the door: 'maybe if I show that I know vaguely what I'm talking about, she might let us in' ... with Anjali beside me I talk about Jeff and Joy and as I do I begin to realize how soft and slippery what I actually remember really is. The woman is friendly, she smiles and yet she says: 'no ... no, it wasn't like that ...' and then what she goes on to says sounds just like what I'd said!!

'Er ... I ... er ... uhh ... uh ...'

I try one last time to make a rope from all this sand. I can see through the big front window that there's a larger communal front room. I remember, or I think I remember, evenings in a room like this.

'If we could just come in for a moment, I might be able to remember something ...'

'I've got to go to Cash and Carry.'

She's polite, but she drops her head to one side.

And I was in that childhood again – not the secure and warm one – but the humiliated one.

When the door was shut and we had escaped from the drive, we laughed and laughed. And I knew I'd got a good bit for this performance. But I knew the whole point of it had fallen off into the sea and it was all about something else now.

I emailed Anjali a little while after we'd finished our walking together ... I'd realized those crab shells we found, on the banks of the Teign, they weren't the casualties of any gulls – they were old shells left behind by crabs that'd slipped out of them and slid away to harden into new versions of themselves!

I left my shell behind ... the Crowhurst boat on the Cayman Islands beach.

'Tat tvam asi.'

That's how you are.

[*After the performance hand out maps/mis-guides for the audience's own exploring around the routes of the performance.*]

Notes
1. This paragraph was eventually cut for performance.
2. Frederick Thomas, *Poetic Pictures, Legends and Stories of Devon* (London: Kent and Co., 1883), p. 7.
3. Arthur L. Salmon, *West Country Ballads and Verses* (Edinburgh: William Blackwood & Sons, 1849), p. 20.
4. Nicholas Tomalin and Ron Hall, *The Strange Voyage of Donald Crowhurst* (London: Hodder & Stoughton, 1970), p. 30.
5. This passage was eventually cut for performance.

Phil Smith performing *The Crab Walks*. Photo: Anne-Maree Garcia.

CRAB WALKING AND MYTHOGEOGRAPHY

Phil Smith

Story

A few years ago I 'chose' to walk. Before then walking had been a function of something else: getting to work, to the cinema, collecting the children from nursery. Walking outside of this functionality was to enter others in disguise: health, leisure. 'Strolling' was tiresome.

Even as I moved from making plays for theatre-designated spaces to site-specific performances – working with Wrights & Sites from 1997 – travel to, from and about their sites remained stubbornly functional.[1] I might have made the leap to 'site', but I had dragged the limitations of the theatre with me. Landscape as backdrop. Unexpected events and appearances barely acknowledged. I sought familiarity in sites analogous to studios and theatres. Upsets and alarms while working on the *Pilot Navigation* part of Wrights & Sites' *The Quay Thing* (1998) sent me running for cover.[2] I had yet to understand that a site might – and might be encouraged to – perform.

In discussions about *The Quay Thing* within Wrights & Sites, our enjoyment of the initial explorations of our sites began to stand out from the performances in them. A site's own performativity was something I began to take seriously. We debated how a process – in which porous sites had begun to close up and people who had welcomed us had backed off – might be reversible. The theatricality onto which I had clung in anxiety began to show itself as a distraction. I began to generalize about the opportunities of site-specificity rather than make particular excuses for having missed them. Without Wrights & Sites I doubt if I would have followed through the implications of these reactions.

The result was an aesthetic practice of walking. This walking began as an anti-theatrical act, and while elements of theatricality have resurfaced in its practice, that tension remains. And interdependency too: for the site-based performances of Wrights & Sites revealed places to be as performed as the performances in them. This understanding – at first as a problem to be removed – would eventually inform the development of walking into something more tactical.

Preparing for *The Quay Thing* had been gruelling, overfull with surprises: quiet canal banks would suddenly erupt with drunken Land Rovers, local soldiers would become enthused and want to see 'the whole film', the roar of passing express trains would overwhelm text, the stink from a pet food factory would infiltrate everything synaesthetically – these were moments when the sites would perform at the expense of and despite the performance. It took a long time to realize that this *was* the performance. This *was* the specificity. And that the site-artist's work was simply to provoke these specificities, to accelerate their decay, to destabilize their poise. And that we should only make the performances that 'performed us', not importing themes or fictions, but at most our associations, memories, misunderstandings: *our* mythogeographies just like those of our sites.

After *The Quay Thing* my first response was to retreat from these challenges, hiding from public spaces in more controllable private ones, creating *Bubbleworld* (1999) for my back garden. Parallel to my own retreat, Wrights & Sites were working out the consequences of these difficult experiences and part of this, crucially, was the organizing of a 'drift', an exploratory wander partly inspired by the situationist journeying theorized by Guy Debord. The first suggestion for this seems to have come from Simon Persighetti during a highly fractious meeting. My retreat from public sites and the neo-Symbolist theatrical qualities of the pieces I was presenting as Wrights & Sites satellite performances had created disquiet. In the debris of an alcohol-fuelled debate about site-specificity the positive suggestion for some sort of non-performance-based exploration, a reassertion of site, had been made.

> Could we not really derive, i.e. drift?
> Could that not include a fairly spontaneous mix of buses and walking?
> …I don't want to do a performance as such – not in an overt way, anyway.
> Could we carry things like chalk, bread crumbs, icing sugar and leave trails?
> (Email from Cathy Turner, 21 November 1999)

It was necessary, certainly for me, to be forced to move further from theatre before I could begin to grasp the theatricality of sites themselves.

Granule

> 19th December was also a chance to test out some of the thinking that had developed from my earlier, opportunistic (mis)use of the word 'mythogeography' – this had led us, via 'psychogeography', the writing of Iain Sinclair, the work of Mike Pearson and his

Re:bus Drift, Exeter, UK, Wrights & Sites (2000). Photo: Phil Smith.

walks/performances, and much much else, to the situationists' 'dérive' or 'drift' – a spontaneous and playful travelling and research through cities, seeking out those spaces where ambience resists the imperatives and spectacle of capital; seeking through a process of détournement (the redeployment of sclerotic art forms) to make 'situations', locations where people can make experiments in new ways of urban living. At least that's what I thought I was partly trying to do. It was almost certainly very different for everyone else.

(from Phil Smith, Re:Bus, document distributed privately, 2002)

Re:Bus was the first of many walkings that I began to infuse with the exploratory and contrary qualities that both 'rough' and neo-Symbolist theatres had previously held for me, discovering that at a distance from theatre I could still engage with the performativities of particular aesthetic forms, an aggressive 'détournement' being an effective motor for reclaiming the remnants of these historical forms. I found I was freer, more autobiographical and no longer isolated in the process of making. At the same time, there was a search for generalities: for categories of space, for geometrical forms, for a vocabulary of atmospheres, as much a wander through ideals and ideological motions as an excavation of granular, highly textured, particle-like, component properties and events.

The following passage – from a privately distributed documentation of a series of drifts – suggests just how granular the experience of a drift could be:

Another dread space appears unexpectedly on a diversion from gothic spaces; the tops of Little Haldon, 60 years-disused aerodrome, obsolete sign 'Dangerous Boar Running', deglazed skeletal remains of the 30s Violet industry, St Nectan's at Ashcombe dedicated to a decapitated martyr foxgloves growing from his blood, the farm that ate a bishop's palace, the red-eyed black wisht-hounds, heard but never seen, guilty Saxon memories of doing nothing as Athelstan's men came for their Celtic neighbours, a former observatory that houses Hitler's private telephone, an unravelling planet on its lawn, Bishop Grandisson sending a raping, murdering priest to lonely Lidwell Chapel. Now ruined, one standing gloom wall looms like a one-eyed monster...

(from Phil Smith, *A Year of Walking*, document distributed privately, 2004)

Into this swirl of detail, of something like local history, of rubble and rubbish and of disrupted expectations, the autobiographical and the neo-Platonic 'world' of ideal forms were plunged together, both part of the currents and the navigators of them. The term 'mythogeography' had been embraced by Wrights & Sites as a shorthand for our resistance to the monocular-identity manufactured by Tourist Boards and Local Councils: a pseudo-discipline that equally values unbuilt proposals, murders, victims, lies and rumours, subjective associations, places of intense atmosphere, lost histories, unusual sightings, gossips, ghosts, diaphanous traces of the secret state, reserve collections, library stacks, wormholes, old signage that has become hieroglyphic and the banal details of mass production as much as any official historiography.

Drifting alone, Prangins, Switzerland (2003).

But I was trying to push the category further, first as a set of general principles and second as an accumulative practice.

I sought out alternatives, complementary or otherwise, to situationist theory – in science and pseudo-science, in esoterica, in arts and literatures, and in other practices of disrupted walking. I found traces of a culturally sensitized, astute walking among early twentieth-century 'trampers', who were using tramping as a conscious disrupting of regular lives ('Tramping is first of all a rebellion against housekeeping … You may escape from the spending mania …') and keen to resist such regularizing of their walks ('Mile averages are a curse. So are definite programmes').[3] In the case of Stephen Graham, there was both an avoidance of the romantic imposition on the landscape ('imagination, though very charming, is nearly always wrong. Knowledge of living detail shows the world to be full of the unexpected, the unanticipated, the unimagined')[4] and an awareness of the possibility of transforming walking itself by taking routes that disrupted the uses of the built environment and the functionality of the walking:

> There is a type of tramping which belongs to the future; a new type, and an even more fascinating one, and that is the taking of cross-sections of the world, the cutting across all roads and tracks, the predispositions of humdrum pedestrians, and making a sort of virginal way across the world.[5]

Graham's description of 'tramps' (walks) in London are similar to accounts of psychogeographic 'drifts'. He is super-democratic, while articulating the materiality of ideological forces at work in geographies: 'Civilisation … is not familiar with its own ground plan.[…] Maps ought to be free for all […]. Wall-maps are busy studying you while you are thinking of other things. You are reading the *Arabian Nights* but Arabia is reading you'. As with maps so with the mapped: '… put no destination label on your rucksack […]. You are not choosing what you shall see in the world, but are giving the world an even chance to see you'.[6] I have been influenced by this displacing of the 'eye' of the walker. In *The Crab Walks*, I give the audience modelling clay to make a head for carrying while walking. Similar to the hindu *Darshana*, looking becomes an active, material force.

Inspired by Graham's urban walking another 'tramper' of the time, Geoffrey Murray, saw the novelty, at least, of a gaze being turned on itself:

> I believe that a new walk, which will develop … is the zoological walk. The great game reserves of the world will shortly be as accessible to an Englishman as Whipsnade is today to anyone living in, say, Southampton … And at the other extreme will come, I predict, the development of walks undertaken in pursuit of the 'Natural History of Streets'. This is a study full of possibilities. There are as many interesting characters to be met in the back-streets of cities as in the tap-rooms of country inns …[7]

While Murray's 'new walk' is deeply compromised, transferring a colonial zoology to an exercise in class similar to 'slumming', what is interesting is an exoticizing of the 'everyday', equally and contemporaneously present in the work of neo-Romantic writer Arthur Machen, author of *The London Adventure* or *The Art of Wandering* whose work is filled with places dissonant with 'dread', researched through his exploratory walking:

> [H]e who cannot find wonder, mystery, awe, the sense of a new world and an undiscovered realm in the places by the Gray's Inn Road will never find those secrets elsewhere, not in the heart of Africa...'The matter of our work is everywhere present' wrote the old alchemists...All the wonders lie within a stone's throw of King's Cross Station.[8]

These nodes of esoteric abstraction, empirical science deeply compromised by its oppressive involvement in space and place and the complicit empire of the everyday, racked with contradictions of the democratic and the exotic, are the crossed spaces in which I began to sense a tainted and barely self-aware tradition that might be sufficiently diaphanous to claim for mythogeography.

To these phenomena I would subsequently add the landscape paintings of Paul Nash, the colours of Powell and Pressburger, the morbid locations of Romero movies, the Prague/non-Prague of Gustav Meyrink, Alfred Kubin and Paul Leppin, the Budapest/non-Budapest of Géza Csáth, my own Bely-inspired walks down the Nevsky Prospect in 1990 and 1991, and similarly spatialized and desperate attempts to 'catch up' with sciences that I had ignored 25 years earlier. Now, when walking, these sciences began to bathe my field of vision with spectral geometries of optic array, Clifford Algebras, extended organisms, electro-magnetic fields and quantum entanglements.

The drifts and explorations continued (the re-walkings with others of part of our initial *Re:Bus* drift, three *Z Worlds* walks in search of micro-worlds), interspersed with performances (*Forest Vague Panic* [2001] in my attic continuing the preoccupations of *Bubbleworld*: that is, autobiography and a neo-Symbolist floating of associations). Emphasis was tipped back towards site in collective work with Wrights & Sites: sound-walks; mis-guided tours; a procession; *The Dig* (2000) around Exeter Archaeology's offices and *Textcavation* (2003) in the underground stacks of Exeter's Central Library; and the planning and mobile research for the publication of *An Exeter Mis-Guide* (2003), a disruption of guidebooks and functional walking of the city, and *A Mis-Guide To Anywhere* (2006). This site-based impetus would lead to my own 'Crab Walking' project (2003–06): four weeks of walking along the South Devon Coast feeding a performance, *The Crab Walks* (2004), followed by *Crab Steps Aside* (2005) which would draw on an eclectic mix of drifts from the Channel Islands, Switzerland, around South Devon villages, in München and San Gimignano.

I became increasingly aware, often through the research of other members of Wrights & Sites, that this was all in the context of an exponentially growing interest in the contradictory attractions of the 'anti-art of walking'/'walking as an art practice': *vide* the Company of Vagabonds in Glasgow, Stalker in Rome, Patrick Keiller's films, Anna Best's *Occasional Sights* book of London walking, the 2003 Pre-Amble festival in Vancouver organized by Kate Armstrong, Glowlab's

The conclusion of Writing On The City, Exeter, UK. Wrights & Sites for tEXt Festival (2002).

annual events in New York, Reverend John Davies's pastoral walking in Liverpool, Mike Pearson's *Bubbling Tom* and Dee Heddon's re-walking of it, Raimi Gbadamosi's *The Dreamer's Perambulator*, the work of Lone Twin…and on and on. This eclectic practice, as likely to wander in from architecture, social activism or visual arts as from performance, had gathered sufficient mass to attract its own genealogical traditions into orbits about itself – Rebecca Solnit's *Wanderlust*, Francesco Careri's *Walkscapes* – and to survive happily with its prophets, Long and Fulton, in the wilderness. Rather than to Long's and Fulton's distant adventures, a shakily fulcrum-like position in all this had gone to the situationists whose critiques of tourism and art have both philosophically denied legitimacy to and waved on a self-consciously aesthetic walking.

Praxis

Though few walking artists are true neo-situationists, many selectively raid situationist terminology. The use of 'drift' or 'dérive' to describe exploratory walks, and of 'psychogeography' for both the subconscious of the landscape and its 'mapping', are commonplace. On the other hand, 'spectacle' and 'the critique of everyday life' are rarely cited. Contemporary 'drifters' – both solitary and in groups – may be sympathetic to much of the situationists' social critique, but are nervous of their coruscating history of exclusionary antics. There is little enthusiasm for the revolutionary 'situation'-making to which 'drifts' were intended to lead, nor for the situationists' wider collective organizational aspirations. Indeed, it is to 'everyday life' as en-mythed by de Certeau that many look for a transforming motor, the urban walker re-making the city every day. My own theoretical project – within a mythogeography – is to attempt to match the vicious monopolization of human possibilities described in the situationists' critique of everyday life with exceptional, détourned, disrupted, increasingly patterned and emergent (rather than everyday) 'tactics' necessary for the diffusion of that monopoly, seeking these within (or not far from) the present range of walking and site-related aesthetic practices.

In addressing the disparity between the theoretical hegemony of the situationists and the actual practices of contemporary walking artists, rather than advocating a more persuasive narrative to replace the situationists' Leftism, I suggest increasing the theoretical and technical ideas in orbit. Not a clarification, but a dynamic/theatrical mapping of the present orbits (predominantly around 'drift' and 'psychogeography') simultaneously occurring with the introduction of new bodies, theoretical and empirical, respectable and non-respectable, into these existing planetary-like motions.

'As above so it is below.' As in theory so in practice. The following passage from a privately distributed documentation of a series of drifts, drawn upon for both *The Crab Walks* and *Crab Steps Aside*, illustrates the ways in which the drift itself involves the same diffusion of authority and planning as in mythogeographical theory and the same setting of different and contradictory elements in motion about each other in order to confront patterns of meaning usually invisible to physically static contemplation. Here, also, is the necessity for autobiography: the artist-walker must set self and route in motion through the shapes and the narratives of the landscape, each threatening the others with dissolution in the acceleration of their interactions. In the practice of the 'drift' and, metaphorically, in the motion of mythogeographic theory, the subjective loses its authority, unleashing the everyday from its industrialization into eccentricity (literally 'standing up'), releasing pleasure into a socialized 'whirl'.

Eleanor e-mails me two days after the walk:

> I slept like the proverbial log on Sunday night and didn't dream at all but last night had a kaleidoscopic melange of images from the walk.

> We were all in the chapel and, wherever someone stood, behind them the chapel was complete, presumably as it originally was, and bathed in light, but as I looked around it was decayed, as we saw it, everywhere else. Then when I looked at someone else it was complete behind them, etc. So it was a bit like a trip through time with each of us being the catalyst for making the chapel come back to life – or death – very weird. But it was very light and vibrant...

But this is not the place, this leads to the place – because I have lost 'control' of the walk there is possibility. This is someone else's map, approaching Lidwell Farm, it's trespass now, I go up to a knee in soft mud, I drop back, I'm expecting a farm dog, the necessary low-level paranoia for exploring is kicking in, a huge arse-up portentous dead sheep rots at the edge of the field. We are all silent. The farmyard is deserted, a piece of the redolent chapel jigsawed mistakenly into a barn wall, cheat, hybrid, things start to swirl, spaces exchange places – and here it is, dread in a barn, sheep listening blank-faced to swing music – everything feels very grey inside my eyes, outside the light at the end of a rainy day is turning the greens and browns of fields into rich dirty 1950s colour, of *Vertigo* and *Marnie*, a dead lamb on the other side of the murky hedge, there is something of the Dionysian mediation of female and male, the gendered leading and led of the drift, the disruption of definitions and identities. More farmhouses all painted in identical Hoare, East India money, gleaming dull like crime scenes as if they had some agency, as early Corman films, appearing to Robert Smithson 'with a "gleaming and ghastly radiance" (Poe) ... seem not to exist at all except as spectral cinematic artifices. The menacing fictions of the terrain engulf the creatures that pass for actors ...',[9] deflecting on us creatures, engulfed by tumultuous rain, 'an ecstatic, godlike freedom from the fixity of character' despite the un-sought desertion and decay; what Lesley Wade (Soule) calls 'a dangerous carnival'.[10] As the last vestige of 'led' walk dissolves, the slipperiness of the memetic complex of 'self' is itself set in slithery motion, its history of risk in the mixing of other personae, characters, masks and, now, place.[11] The worship of Dionysus was associated with remote places; the memetic power 'behind' the mask of the god continuing to exert a mutable, mutating force, even when the last mask is unravelled and there is no beyond.

(from *A Year of Walking*, document privately distributed, 2004)

Then from the text of *The Crab Walks*, the same site and the same issues:

The Monk would lure women here, rob them and throw their bodies down the well. Or he would disguise himself as a traveller and rob the wealthy. Or he was a child-murderer from another place. Or a rapist from Gidley. Or he was a clerk whose ideas were unorthodox. Or was thrown down his own well by a devout sailor who raising his eyes to heaven saw the monk's shadow, knife in hand, on the chapel wall [*Me to mime the shadow, facing the audience, fingers flickering for the gulls' wings*] – flickering like gulls across a pavement. [*Drop hand to side.*] Or he is a jumbled memory of the violence to the chapel itself – by men of puritan religion who hated the voluptuous curve of an image. [*Making curved S with hand. Then, distorting my own voice and body.*] History stretches and distorts him like some kind of monster! The place is pulled and bent in the same way. In 1980 a photograph taken of the ruins, when developed, revealed a complete chapel. The photograph has since disappeared.

In *The Crab Walks* and *Crab Steps Aside*, I set out to place the autobiographical in an instrumental role, as the emotional motor for destabilizing the assumed, as a diffusion, not for its own sake, but one that allowed me to dismantle certain narratives and ideas before an audience, and as a rhetoric for encouraging them to disrupt themselves and diffuse their own dismantling. The performances sought to challenge the authenticity of their own autobiographical voice. In both pieces I often say that I cannot remember things, that strong emotional memories evaporate in the face of their supposed sites, that what I felt most strongly mine came to feel alien and shared.

There are many different 'voices' in the performances. I am conversational sometimes, academic sometimes, friendly, intensely engaged, relaxed; at times I'm story-telling and at other times lecturing, imitating (inventing) the voices of others met on my walks, and when I 'act' myself I already set up a paradox. Many audience members remarked on these different voices. Significantly, after the performances almost no one asked questions about the directly autobiographical elements. I can only remember one: did my fighter pilot/rally driver father mind having an artist for a son? Almost every other conversation would begin with something about people's own walking or some place they had found, a panther and a wallaby sighted in the Midlands, a piece of magical cork from Combeinteignhead that brought good luck at bingo to a relative … it was the mythogeography, rather than the autobiography that was elaborated.

But it was not the silencing of the autobiographical that I was after: rather the mythologizing of it. And not my own in particular, but anyone's. To bring the autobiographical into a play of generalities.

There is a model for this process in the seventeenth-century utopian romance *The Blazing World* written by Margaret Cavendish, Duchess of Newcastle. In the romance the Duchess appears as herself in spirit form, and is asked by the fictional Empress of the Blazing World for assistance in devising a Cabbala. Advising the Empress against scriptural, philosophical, moral or political Cabbalas, the Duchess-Spirit proposes: 'rather to make a poetical or romantical Cabbala, wherein you can use metaphors, allegories, similitudes, etc. and interpret them as you please'. When the Duchess's spirit and the Empress become Platonic lovers, the Duchess longs for her own empire, but is advised by fellow spirits: '[W]e wonder...that you desire to be Empress of a terrestrial world, whereas you can create your self a celestial world if you please?...every human can create an immaterial world'.[12]

'It's the way you link the little things to the big picture,' someone said after a performance.

Pattern
So what is this 'big picture'?

It is physical in the sense of the discipline of Physics rather than in that of its objects, conceptual, but geometrical more than theoretical. It challenges 'text' as the primary articulation of the 'general'. It is the re-assertion of a sort of haunted super-empiricism. It is linked to a Kantian sublime, to an ecological theory of perception, to an 'evolution' in which forms leap across species and from non-living to living matter as described by Bachelard ('stones that imitate a jaw-bone...Orchis, Diorchis...which imitate the male organs. [...] Here names think and dream ... mineralogical [and horticultural] collections are anatomical parts of what man will be when nature learns to make him...form is the habitat of life')[13] and to Roger Penrose's 'feeling that the mathematics to describe these things [the relation of the physical world to mentality, our ability to access mathematic truth] is out there' and to his 'prejudice[s]...that the entire physical world can, in principle, be described in terms of mathematics [...]. Thus, there is a small part of the Platonic World which encompasses our physical world'.[14] More prosaically it is sometimes an interpretation of scale or sequence: Paul Nash's observation that 'there was a peculiar spacing in the dispersal of the trees...which suggested some inner design of very subtle purpose'.[15]

This 'picture' is constructed knowingly and theatrically. The forms and worlds described become characters in the 'picture', players even, houses once seen in a forest that cannot be found again, imaginary islands, the country of Hi-Brazil only ever seen in mirages. This is an idealized conceptualizing of what will later reappear, in a making of 'situations', as the provocation of the city to 'perform itself'.

This is not a simple philosophical formalism, but one haunted by empirically observed, often invisible, physical processes. For example, the human eye is continuously scanning for the extra-sensitivity of its photoreceptors when aligned with the Earth's magnetic field, or the tiny temperature fluctuations in the microwave background. Minute wrinkles from the very early universe that correspond to the great galactic structures, these are maps of the cosmos continually passing through our bodies. These patternings can be walked – spectrally, theatrically – the walker 'carrying' such and similar empirical patterns (satellite capture dynamics, astronomical precession) not as text, not as idea even, but as their own theatrical stage, the walker able to mentally unroll this 'tragic carpet' of patterns wherever s/he needs.[16]

This 'staging' chimes with a growing 'formalist' tendency in the physical (which crosses, transgressively, to the social) sciences: the mathematical biology advocated by Evelyn Keller Fox; the organic, inorganic and social patterns in the multi-disciplinary work of Philip Ball; the 'Li' of David Wade, a concept that 'falls between our notions of pattern and principle'.[17] This tendency has become a formalism of forms in the work of J.A. Scott Kelso and others: 'to understand the ways nature has devised to compress billions of (potential) degrees of freedom into a few functionally relevant macroscopic quantities'.[18] A patterning or dynamism of patterns, basic pattern-forming principles that operate whatever the scale, is something Scott Kelso ties explicitly to Penrose's claim of real-world materiality for mathematical concepts: 'This is what I mean when I propose that the linkage across levels of description in complex systems is by virtue of shared dynamical principles'. But when it comes to consciousness Scott Kelso throws his net wider than Penrose's theory of consciousness as a quantum effect in the brain's microtubules: 'globality of thought emerges ... as a conscious, self-organised property of the nervous system coupled, as it is, to the environment'.[19]

Although Scott Kelso has some trouble with will and intention (perhaps because his patterns are informational ones), he does his best to null the off-putting whiff of pre-determinism. While 'fluctuations' continuously probe his systems, simultaneously articulating their stabilities and their options for new patterns, change occurs when order parameters (those patterns governing the relations of the system's different parts) become unsettled. Crucially for our application here, critical fluctuations anticipate upcoming pattern change. So, rather than looking to particular parts of a system, it is to its pattern of relations that we should look for changeability.

But why should 'we'? Isn't this the remnants of my personal trajectory through socially engaged Christianity, grassroots community and council tenants' activism, the Bennite left of the 1980s and the international socialism of the Socialist Workers Party projected onto an imagined 'we', positioned by me on my new playground of space? This questionable conflating is part of the grounds for the necessity of autobiography that I am struggling with, advocating, but not resolving, here. And because this is not a 'one cause-one effect system' the role of the subjective is important here, for the provocation to change can be out of all proportion to its effects.

'In self-organising systems, a small change, say, in the temperature gradient applied to a fluid can produce a huge collective shift'.[20] In a complex, self-organizing system like a city this means that a small provocation, when deployed sensitively, to the ongoing fluctuations in the city can generate a disproportionate response. René Thom uses the *metaphor* of quantum tunnelling (in which particles that lack the energy to 'climb' the brow of a process 'tunnel' through to their objective) to suggest how such a disproportionate mechanics might work, related *as if* to an organism

> resting in a ground state, a local minimum surrounded by basins of attraction that possess ever deeper minima corresponding to excited states. The perception of a pregnant form (say prey) creates a tunnel effect, switching the animal into an excited state. Once the prey is caught and eaten, satisfaction lifts the basin of attraction.[21]

The changes here involve very small transfers of energy, because these are patterns of information rather than force, just as off-course satellites with minimal propulsion resources have been successfully transferred from one orbit to another by 'playing' their low 'card' just at the point where the entanglement of extremely powerful gravitational forces will yield a disproportionate effect. It is mostly the *understanding* of the dynamic patterns at work that 'causes' change. In order, then, for equivalent social patterns to be successfully provoked, it requires artists or anti-artists who are 'informed' in the non-empirical patterns (basins) of attraction in their city or society and who are able to appropriately deploy the small transfers of energy to provoke the 'sinking' of a basin or tunnelling to an existing basin necessary to trigger the city/system to change, particularly – to follow this model – when the tunnelling is to an attraction that cannot be easily satisfied. This is the return of a situationist strategy, a provocation of site working itself along the continuum of theatrical site-specificity to its most radical edge: goading the city (or rural system) into 'performing itself'.

Along another continuum it is a movement from Arthur Machen to Homi Bhabha, from an esoteric peeling away of appearance ('even these vile red stones (bricks) may be transmuted into living, philosophical stones')[22] to a political 'daemonic doubling' (Bhabha echoing Wade [Soule]) in which, referencing Conrad,

German Occupation Underground Hospital, Guernsey. Photo: Phil Smith.

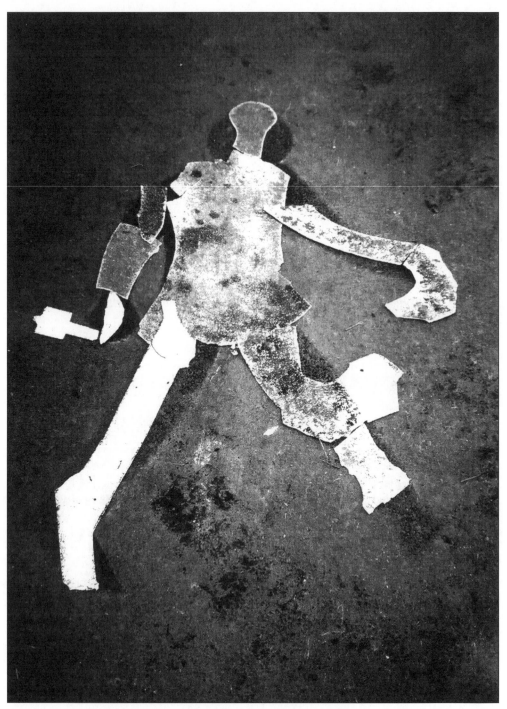

Détourned pathway sign, Hoopern Valley Path, Exeter, UK. Photo: Phil Smith.

the local story of love and its domestic memory can only be told between the lives of history's tragic repressions...the street of tall houses takes on the profile of the tribal skulls on staves; the percussive pounding of a heart echoes the deep beat of drums [...]. Between the silent truth of Africa and the salient lie to the metropolitan woman...the 'chaos' that afflicts the signification of psychic and historical narratives in racialized societies.[23]

There is nothing simple here, no passing from one world to another, but a complex entanglement of history, a cultural version of what Einstein referred to in quantum non-locality as 'spooky action at a distance', the disproportions and silences of which situation-making seeks to use to provoke the city.

Here, if you like, is the meta-narrative of the Crab Walking project – of 'crab walkers' experiencing through their 'drifts' the informational non-linear dynamics of the predominantly self-organizing urban or rural system *and* its wormholes (these Bhabha-ian gaps between the silence and the lie), in order to provoke radical site-specified performances, not by the 'crab walkers', but by the city of the city, by the town of the town.

Screen

The theatricality of the cities performing of themselves has a doppelganger on the 'drift': cinema. In the *Crab* performances, on 'drifts' and in maps, I evoke cinema locations and 'moments' regularly – the dread space of the pier from Herk Harvey's *Carnival of Souls* (1962), the perspective of the gulls in Hitchcock's *The Birds* (1963) – as a sublime; non-human in scale, with threatening implications for the autobiographical.[24]

So what of human agency in these patterned 'fields' and cinematic bathings? What for the situation-maker rather than the psychogeographer? A cinema-sublime offers a model for a provocative inscrutability that is, ironically, perhaps best referenced in drama: the Khlestakov of Gogol's *The Government Inspector*. Khlestakov creates disproportionate reactions not by intentions, but by absenting them, avoiding them. My repeated references to cinema are an attempt to evoke just such a dual presence of action and inscrutability, the blankness of the screen 'originated as a necessary absence, a condition of erasure, clearing, which makes possible...the maximum mobility of the sign'.[25] In the making of 'situations', a cinematic-Khlestakovian inscrutability is unlikely to be arrived at immediately. Provocation must usually itself be provoked initially (see the tactics of Simon Persighetti below) but then may become inscrutable, 'systematic', emergent.

Motion

The *motion* of the 'drift' is crucial. The 'drifter' needs a sensitivity both to the motion of the landscape through which they move and to the pattern of their senses in motion. Cultivating such a sensibility enables the 'drifter' to recognize dynamic non-linear patterns in their own perception; patterns indicative of disproportionate change, in the body as in the city.

James J. Gibson's ecological theory of perception was derived from experiments on subjects in motion (pilots, etc.) and is based on the ideas that in the environment 'certain higher-order variables of stimulus energy – ratios and proportions, for example – do *not* change' and that continuous perception is based on the ability of an individual to detect these invariants.[26] There is no mediation of these invariants in perception – 'the whole system of input and output resonates to the external information' – so the senses operate not so much as receptors but 'analogous to tentacles and feelers',[27] like the active looking of *Darshana*. Perception is a 'loop' that includes the invariants in the ecology and the activity of the whole body. What it 'feels' for is information: 'analysed by forms, not by points',[28] not by energy, but relations.

In Gibson's theory, both subjects and objects are active: 'the optic array...not only provided bare information but also offered possibilities for action on the basis of that information'. These possibilities were called 'affordances' by Gibson: 'neither an objective fact about the environment nor a subjective idea in the mind. It cuts right across the old subjective-objective divide..."both physical and psychical, yet neither" to use Gibson's own words'.[29] Here, in perceptual research, the psychological and the geographical in psychogeography are affirmed as a deferred synthesis: ambience as the deferral of the synthesis of information in the environment with subjective experience of that environment. Atmospheres 'exist' both objectively and subjectively, yet as neither subjects nor objects.

In order to become aware of such deferred patternings in the material environment, Gibson suggested fixating on a single point, then 'pay(ing) attention not to that point...but to the whole range of what you can see, keeping your eyes still fixed. The attitude you should take is that of the perspective draughtsman [...]. This is...the visual field'. When 'drifters' walk with an awareness of this 'visual field', rather than the visual world ('the familiar, ordinary scene of daily life in which solid objects look solid'),[30] they become aware that it is clear only at its centre, that it is curved at its edges and that the curved areas straighten when the eyes are turned towards them, that parts of their face are represented in that field. The visual world is 'unsettled' in the 'visual field'; it becomes liquifacted, its granular, apparently discrete parts are set in flow, put in doubt. Commodity and property become, apparently, malleable.

In the texts of *The Crab Walks* and *Crab Steps Aside* there are evocations of this unsettling patterned or spatial looking: for example, in describing the reported sightings of anomalous big cats in the United Kingdom, I refer to the shape of *Dinofelis*, a generic hunter of humans of 2,500,000 years ago, imprinted on the contemporary mind: 'As far as templates go, one needn't think in terms of something like a silhouette that looks cat-like. There could be, for example, certain kinds of motion cues that trigger the impression of a predator'.[31] Such destabilized patterned looking is implicit in the maps created with Tony Weaver and distributed at *Crab Steps Aside* performances: a distorted grid for the *Angel Drift*, a pseudo-geological cross-section for the Haldon Hills.

The drifter *in motion*, triggered by fixation, self-consciously aware of the 'visual field', can use such perceiving as a means to overcome the commodification of the city in packages of exchange:

the ability to see from (another) point of view, depends on being oriented in space. Orientation is inseparable from locomotion, for, only because an observer gets a different visual field at every different standpoint, does he perceive a single integrated world.[32]

Thus the conscious use of the visual field restores the city to the imaginary possibility of the situationists' 'unitary urbanism...in which separations such as work/leisure or public/private will finally be dissolved'[33] through a synthesis of 'arts and techniques' in the creation of mutating ambiences. Using the 'visual field' and a grasp of dynamic nonlinearity, the 'drifter' seeks out 'functionally relevant macroscopic' patterns, negotiating the billions of possibilities in the unbounded perceptual world. Using this mix of intellect and intuition the drifter 'feels' for the tipping points in the city and in her/his own perception.

[O]ur brain...is poised on the brink of instability where it can switch flexibly and quickly. By living near criticality, the brain is able to anticipate the future, not simply react to the present.[34]

The sustained motion of the 'drift' enables the dériviste to begin to pattern the city's tipping points, adding to the perception of atmospheres the spectre of dynamic patterns.

But there is a need here, amid all this talk of patterns, to retain something like 'intuition' in order to defer a synthesis of all these elements to a single objective explanation, a need to push to the edge of chaos where change in systems lurks. Only by instability – 'irrationality' – in the system is it possible to anticipate the future effects of small transfers of energy on an open complex system. This is what is acknowledged when the US military call in Hollywood screenwriters to anticipate Al Qaeda's next move: their suspicion that the qualitative leap of 9/11 was informed by *Independence Day*. This is what drives the pop-cultural/esoteric/pseudo-scientific layer of my 'drifting': the belief that the political/economic layer is as likely to be fuelled by fragments of half-believed narratives about 'invasions', 'epidemics' and 'devils' as by 'rational' discourses *about* economics and politics.

Site

As my concern grew with an 'anywhere' that was 'both physical and psychical, but neither', the dark, bounded and intimate space of the beach huts in which I had performed *The Crab Walks* (so close to the audience that Anjali Jay, 'outside eye' for *The Crab Walks*, remarked that my body became the map of my journeys) was exchanged for a range of performance sites for *Crab Steps Aside*. The parameters of the beach huts were controllable. The tiny audiences sat with their backs to the door. Occasionally an audience member might turn to simultaneously look at the landscape and listen to the stories. In *Crab Steps Aside* I experimented with giving everyone this option, using outdoor sites (by the side of the Teignmouth Lido, a field overlooking the River Teign, on a viewing platform above Coryton Cove, on a Dawlish tea shop patio open to the sky) and more inscribed, more cluttered indoor ones like Dawlish Museum's 'industrial room' or ones with large views (a bar with a view of bowling green and cliff, a room looking to sea on one side and disused cinema on the other). I was trying to challenge the primacy of the story-telling text with the play of the sites in which I performed and by silent movement sequences devised with Sue Palmer, who acted as 'outside eye' for *Crab Steps Aside*. After a performance at Coryton Cove an audience member remarked on the layers of site: the 'real' but absent sites that I described becoming 'present' while the vista behind and around us seemed both present and bathed by the performance's acted-ness.

In *Crab Steps Aside* I was also pushing my own presence towards a rhetorical, exemplary one: attempting to model the 'drift' in the manner of a story-telling 'in site'. Tim Ingold's description of 'ordinary wayfinding' as 'closely resembl(ing) storytelling' turns this around, while accurately describing my feelings while performing *Crab Steps* in these open sites:

> the traveller... 'feels his way' towards his goal, continually adjusting his movements in response to an ongoing perceptual monitoring of his surroundings... the unfolding of a field of relations established through the immersion of the actor-perceiver within a given environmental context.[35]

I was, in hope, edging toward a variegated practice in which space and generality are not layers 'above' the particular, but specific and sited practices that take their chances with all the others; an encouragement that everyone should be a theorist, take their own ideas seriously, test their generalities against their actions, site their own 'little things' in 'big pictures'.

In this way it is not autobiography making us exceptional and individual, rather it is the 'to', the 'in motion', the 'about' of what is individual that is revealed and practiced: our autobiographical motion. The stories from audience members after the performances – of resonant vistas, routes, seasonal changes, strange beasts half-seen – will only be 'placed' by their own 'drifts', theoretical and practical. (Hence the essentially rhetorical nature of these two shows: to give 'feeling' to the idea of a practice.)

Just as architectural ruins are bathed in the frisson of our own decay still to come, so an enjoyment of the self's destabilization/contortion can be projected, playfully, into a utopia. The ruins of self evoke the possibilities of everything else – autobiography made mythical, made mythogeographical. Space, place, environment, route and way are not passive surfaces for traversal nor blank pages on which the active walker writes nor accomplished texts awaiting reading, but are active: both psychical and physical, but also something that is neither. They are 'characters' that the 'drifter' seeks to provoke into performances of themselves, through the rearrangement of signs, the placing of objects, the carrying of 'burdens', the leaving of messages, the re-constructing of rubbish-heaps: theatricalities that, in turn, theatricalize quotidian behaviours around them, re-performing space into something resistant to the intentions of its planners, designers and controllers.

Another provocation is playfulness. It sets off a political reaction: the a-functionality of play offers no 'real' threat to the functions of the space, but as the antithesis of these functions the managers of space often seem 'forced' to 'take it seriously', to shadow the frivolity of the 'player'. In doing so these controllers are forced to 'play' their roles in order to hang onto them; they speak their subtexts, expose their training, their orders, their own psychogeographies: so Wrights & Sites have been allowed to play on artificial ski slopes, been assured that broom cupboards are former prison cells, been informed of 'sensitive documents' and police snipers' positions and ejected for lack of the appropriate logo by various managers of space.

Edge

Given the emphasis here on patterns, what of the structure of the *Crab Walks* and *Crab Steps* performances?

In *Crab Walks*, a kind of excavation is proposed: to find the sites of childhood holidays. And yet they no longer are where they were. The performance is a failed archaeology. In *Crab Steps*, the resolution (of a humiliating childhood memory) is only reached by a diffusion, an imagined dying. The parts of the performances are often eating at their overall structure, even from one performance to the other: in *Crab Walks*, empty crab shells are revealed not to be the work of predatory herring gulls (a paranoia about herring gulls had been partly driving the extended *Crab Walks* 'drifting'), but the residue of transformations of the crabs themselves. In *Crab Steps*, however, a found empty crab shell is soft, a dead crab caught mid-transformation, resisting a simple, 'natural' hope. This structuring attempts to follow Bhabha, for whom 'the Third Space of enunciation ... makes the structure of meaning and reference an ambivalent process, destroys the mirror of representation in which cultural knowledge is customarily revealed as an integrated, open, expanding code'.[36] Without recourse to abstruseness, the two texts attempt to disrupt the code, and then each other.

There is a similar uneasiness and auto-dismantling in the act of 'drifting' itself. After a walk using peripheral vision as much as possible, Cathy Turner articulated its unhomeliness:

> Because I was, in a sense, frightened, yes, experiencing a slight feeling of panic, feeling that I was in the grip of Pan's natural wilderness (however cultivated and managed it *actually* was). I had the sense that I was being tricked off the path somehow, that the decision to lose myself was not mine.
>
> (Cathy Turner, private communication, 2003)

Eleanor, Cathy Turner, Anna Best, 'lure(d) women', Rebecca Solnit, Kate Armstrong, *Marnie*, Doreen Massey, Lesley Wade (Soule). Just as women are de-sited by power geometry, can they be provisionally pre-eminent in a de-centred walking that displaces power to the peripheries, one in which the group of walkers, resistant to a manifesto, disposed not to be led, is always fraying at its edges, its boundaries erring to the fractal? Or does the dispersal of the unhomely 'drift' reproduce their disempowerment?

The 'drift' is not a neutral, de-gendered, *tabula rasa* on which all may write equally. But instead, led by its periphery, does the walk become more unpredictable, more edgy? If women are more

Shed Walk, Welcombe, UK (2003). Photo: Phil Smith.

sensitive to movement in their peripheral vision, then are 'edgelands' – the land where urban meets rural, meets economic superfluity unclearly, places towards which 'drifts' often gravitate, defined by Marion Shoard as 'the only theatre in which the real desires of real people can be expressed'[37] – places where women can site themselves more powerfully? Does the drifting group have its own edgelands? Is there something providential in the diffuse walking group in such 'superfluous' space?[38] Much has been written and thought about the 'drifter', the flagrant heir to the un-charismatic *flâneur*, but little about the morphing and eroding of the walking group. A silence that leads – in site-specific performance – to strings of duckling audience trailing after mother-duck performers.

But the periphery *can* lead. For whatever reasons, women were very active in 'leading' the *Shed Walk* procession: the processing of a one-eighth-sized shed, made from the sawn down parts of a whole shed, an event organized by Wrights & Sites for Annabel Other's *Shed Summit* in 2003. The procession began by passing through the arch of the remaining full-sized shed doorway and was, initially, led by me, the carrier of a roof pole with the shed's diamond nailed to the top. I carried the pole to be visible to the 30 or so processors, to launch the procession under its authority, and I very soon wanted to hand it on – and did. Without dispersing, the procession frayed, globules broke off and then rejoined, and its feminized tentacles felt into the nooks and elbow joints of the route, ripples of narration re-cited the site, personal associations circulated, an S&M b&b was identified, at the gateway to a holiday hut one tassel of the procession swept up to a family in their garden, drawing in the miniature shed and the rest of us, swarming, welcomed, for a few minutes of posing and photographs and a remarkably relaxed address by the surprised shed-owner. None of this occurred in the political economy of the situationist metropolis, but in superfluous spaces.

This fraying of authority becomes, by necessity, exploratory, but is equally necessarily fraught with disturbance. Peripheral vision of a sudden motion prompts rapid signals to an early evolved part of the brain that in turn prompts physical evasive action: a pre-emptive physical sensitivity at the very edge of the visual frame. The linear certainties of the rambler are denied by the peripheral 'drift'. Even a procession like *Shed Walk* becomes literally 'edgy' – even more so the walk cited by Cathy Turner, on an isolated estate wandering for hours. Walking becomes disorienteering, its internal uncertainty offering, at worst, opportunities for a re-development of power geometries.

Lodge

While working on a joint paper for the 2005 Altered States Conference (Plymouth, United Kingdom), with the mathematician and 'drifter' Matthew Watkins, Matthew responded to an early draft: 'Who is this "we"?' I had recruited an imaginary collective of 'drifters' to a shared impulse for social change. There is no 'we', but there is a set of networks, of individuals and small groups aware of and sometimes in touch with each other. And there is something more: each group drift becomes a challenge to answer Matthew's question: 'Who is this "we"?'

Three 'drifts' were offered and publicly advertised as part of the *Crab Walks* project – *Dead Fox Drift* around Dawlish, a night walk around Newton Abbot, and the *Wormhole Walk* in and around Combeinteignhead – the latter furnishing the spine narrative for *Crab Steps Aside* –and a further four hybrid presentations/walks jointly organized with Teignbridge Council's Walk This Way project.

The dominant models for group walking are the guided tour and the 'ramble', both of which are most likely to have a leader figure, a destination, a predictable content (views, flora, historic buildings) and a finishing time. Within them there are generally understood roles. Each 'drift' seeks to undermine this: by using the dark (so barely seeing any landscape), by serial structures (walking in groups of diminishing numbers), by its organizer shrugging their shoulders and asking 'Which way?', or by mythogeographical tasks (seeking 'wormholes' to other places or building monuments from discarded rubbish).

Experience uncovers the more obvious ideological traps, but each 'drift' remains to be disrupted, no matter how theoretically astute its walkers. The 'drift' is not a dislocated, pre-existing intellectual or esoteric discipline that can be navigated from level to level of increasing disengagement from or redemption of the fallen world. And yet there are some similarities to the journey of the 'adept'.

The 'drift' group could be compared to a temporary 'lodge', a physical model of an abstracted psyche, like spiritual Freemasonry at its most sincere, engaging with the physicalization of abstractions and their hybridization: 'Geometry, Creation and Travel'. Like Freemasonry, the 'drift' is a rhetorical persuasion – 'the Art by which feeling is introduced into logical and well-structured communication' – and it sees that 'feeling', psychogeographically, as 'hard-wired' into matter:

> the Deity called the relative universe into being so that 'God might behold God' and that the three lower Worlds of Separation were erected … so that Adam Kadmon, the Image of God, might experience all things.[39]

This implies pre-existent patterns (which are dynamic) and a hard-wired human sensibility to them, and defines 'choice' as a cooperation with an existing 'Geometry' rather than a personal development or a humanistic imposition of meaningfulness on a dead world of matter:

> The revival of this, the last school of ancient pagan philosophy, fostered a disposition to blur the difference between matter and spirit. Instead of being regarded as an inanimate mass, the earth itself was deemed to be alive.[40]

By spectralizing this 'Geometry', as both a Platonic 'world' (as mathematics that is 'out there') and an historical esoteric practice involved in radicalism, corruption, female exclusion and conspiracy and wrapped in a miasma of secrets and possibly sinister influences, the 'Geometry' becomes active, its contradictions and gaps analogous to those within which the practice of the mythogeographical 'drift' takes place. So the more experienced 'drifters' can walk and explore a landscape increasingly made symbolic, understanding that those symbols are corrupt (historically) and ideal (radically) in equal parts.

What is going on here? While risking a simple collapse into esotericism – and, indeed, the embarrassment of colleagues – this is an attempt to engage a contemporary memetic and ideological complexity (what Erik Davis has called 'TechGnosis', Marc Augé 'supermodernity' and Jeremy Gilbert-Rolfe 'the techno-sublime') at an earlier, simpler stage, in order to understand its historical nature, but more importantly to be able to use and disseminate a new, re-complexifying of it, rather than allow oneself to be disseminated by it. I am seeking, via a radical nostalgia, in the alchemical beginnings of modern science and the contemporaneous revival of classical ideas, a dynamic model of mind and world. Of such precedents R.J.W. Evans wrote,

> The occult striving was in essence an attempt to penetrate beyond the world of experience to the reality which underlay it, and as such paralleled or overlapped with the artistic use of symbols and emblems. At the same time it belonged in a central way to the whole apprehension of nature.[41]

Here is a contradiction to be treasured: simplistic, manichaeistic, a layering of unreal matter and real spirit, in turn disrupted first by aesthetic symbolism and then drowned by the living nature with which it wrestles.

This cuts against those contemporary social criticisms which seek to reduce the world to passive experience and the dissolution of materiality (including the materiality of that experience), the reduction of place to a supposedly ubiquitous 'non-place', described by Marc Augé as 'a turning back on the self, a simultaneous distancing from the spectator and the spectacle'.[42] The uneven acceleration of Augé's supermodernity in a way lends force to (and changes) Augé's argument, making it more rather than less radical.[43] For this temporal unevenness is symptomatic of a divorce between understanding (and the attempt to understand) and the *spectacle*: those social relations that timetable the conduct of pleasure, systematically (temporally *and* spatially) divorcing thought from ecstasy. This is to pose against the romanticized acceleration of supermodernity a super-nostalgia, radical and disrupted.

In a hostile theoretical and social environment, mythogeography needs nostalgia. Nostalgia's destabilizing qualities can be 'read' in the work of Doreen Massey who at times emphasizes its reactionary features (in *For Space*) and at others (in *Space-time and the Politics of Location*) its ambivalences, articulating in that unevenness just the terrain a mythogeography needs (this is rhetoric, remember?): a field in which the unevenness of a patchy supermodernity and an ambiguous nostalgia can agitate both the sceptical 'drifter' and the ideological timelines of esoterica, spitting up modernism's early, sometimes 'uncharacteristic' memes (future, machismo, theosophy, for example) to be re-contested.

Self

For two years in the mid-1980s I was a paid coordinator for Bristol Broadsides, a community press publishing working-class writers. As a member and coordinator of workshops where autobiographical fragments were regularly presented for discussion and comment, and in

Drifting in Naples, Italy, as a workshop leader at The Present Generation organised by Organic Theatre (2006). Photo: Phil Smith.

regular contact with many of the writers, I became increasingly aware of the 'working' of autobiography, of the sophisticated strategies employed by the most seemingly 'innocent' and 'natural' writer: the editing out of 'disruptive' elements, the creation of organic narrative where there was none, the concentration of narrative into a symbolic language, the arrangement of fragments to create an apparently coherent 'self', the vast silences, the disciplinary narrative embedded in the idea of 'ordinary people with extraordinary stories', the knowing use of certain populist and class 'norms' for the presentation of quite different counter-narratives.

What struck me was not that there were direct untruths (these were generally interchangeable with the facts), but rather the constructedness of any autobiography as well as the intense enjoyment and feelings of release there could be in this re-working of a 'previous life'. The past becomes an alternative incarnation, a 'history' of which the writer becomes the historian, not the authoritative eyewitness of everything and anything, but rather the re-arranger of fragments into quite new patterns. This is radical nostalgia; just as a utopian seeks to make a 'better future' in Nowhere, so the nostalgic returns to the past as if it were Nowhere and rearranges its characters and props in a friction-free non-place where determinations can be re-cast as choices (or mistakes) and accidents as personal qualities (or vices). The I of the autobiography becomes a mythic figure in a mythic landscape.

Coming to the making of my own autobiographical pieces, I was helped by those experiences, spurred to make the structuring and the working as clear as possible, and not to attempt to hide the self-mythologization, but rather to show one element of it (the I/author/walker) openly determined and shaped by another: the geography of its mythicized landscapes. In fact what I made each time was a show about the impossibility of an empirical, mimetic autobiography: 'I' was unfindable and my best shot at myself was imagining my own death, which I then felt, in good taste, I had to deny: 'but that's a lot of nonsense...' The imaginary landscapes I constructed were 'stages' for the denial of subjective discovery, like those guest-houses where I stayed as a child and to which I was denied access as an autobiographical artist. Nor could the everyday, the landscape of my drifts be directly evoked. This was not a simple tale of subjective alienation in reliable spaces.

The situationist critique of everyday life remains as powerful as ever – that, in late capitalism, behaviour is economic and primitive, that the reaction to the fading of scarcity has not been the development of new, sophisticated behaviours or qualities, but rather a quantitative reproduction of survival. Interestingly, this part of situationist theory is little referenced by those influenced by the idea of the dérive. They are much more likely to be attracted to the heroic 'tactics' of the quotidian city dweller championed in de Certeau's version of 'Everyday Life'. But there are problems here. As Doreen Massey points out, de Certeau's 'political imaginary' is of a 'central bloc versus little tactics of resistance... [A]gainst the "city as system", the implacable presence of stabilised legibility, is romanticised a mobile "resistance" of tactics, the everyday, the little people',[44] a binary that hides the way that the 'power geometry' is maintained and refined in the everyday, in the iconic 'street'. Romanticizing 'the streets' can easily lead resistant tactics astray, for example into:

the least politically convincing of situationist capers – getting laddish thrills (one presumes) from rushing about down dark passages, dreaming of labyrinths [...]. (Is this not itself another form of eroticised colonisation of the city?)[45]

Although this is a caricature of urban exploration there is plenty of truth here. Unthinkingly using the everyday as a physicalized virtual home – a 'House of the Dead' without the dead, 'Resident Evil' while the occupants are out – is an escapism explicitly inscribed with all the overproduction of survival long ago fingered in the situationist critique of everyday life. And, as such, urban exploration begs détournement: a potential mythogeographic 'tragic carpet'.

So, there must be a deviation from the quotidian (no matter how exotic or 'underground' that quotidian is), from the return to childhood, from the game playing (which is not to say that any or all these might not be present in a 'drift', but necessarily 'in play' with other critical practices). Equally, any mythogeographical practice is driven, theoretically, to the gaps between respectable and unrespectable, in the consciously navigated flattened banalities of the survival-everyday as disrupted by their own future-filled ruins and accidental wildernesses.

This trajectory is mythical, if nervously so, broadly following the almost theological approach of Hans Jonas:

> [W]ith its invocation of the necessity and desirability of ... a 'tentative myth' ... seeking to show that acceptance of such a theology ... is consistent with ... the apparently godless discoveries of a naturalistic science that conceives reality in terms of contingent, material processes alone.[46]

Where Jonas must have recourse to 'tentative myth' given the weakness of 'god', so both 'drift' and autobiography must have recourse to the same in the face of the weakness of 'self' and 'politics'. The 'tentative myth' is of a semi-heroic, de-Marvelled comic (in both senses) Superwalker that changes what 'e' walks – 'e' because, to borrow from cyberspace at the behest of Sue Thomas,[47] a non-gender, non-known, possibly organic, possibly inanimate, 'e' is the myth/real, collective and imaginary, both psychical and physical, but neither.

This tentatively heroic trajectory is not through or across the site of the everyday, but a trajectory that is the constituent part of the everyday space: a trajectory in places that are constructed of trajectories. Unlike the blank page of space implied by the reading of the city as text, or the emptiness first created by the Gnostic God before filling it with 'fallen' matter, here space is defined by trajectories, as championed by Doreen Massey in For Space. This – i.e. place as trajectories – is a significant refining of Massey's earlier metaphor of a satellite observing place below as a meeting of trajectories. Tim Ingold criticized the reactionary political potential in just this kind of global viewpoint,[48] but in For Space Massey brings the trajectory of the viewpoint into the matrix, making a space that is neither container nor surface. This neither implicates action in the division of form from content, container from contained, nor in the pseudo-colonialist 'taking' of surface (piercing or overwhelming). Action in a space of trajectories is

A global Z world. Z World Drift, Exeter, UK (2003). Photo: Phil Smith.

itself a spacing, implicated and engaged, of the same 'organic' and intellectual material as such space itself. The satellite is now just one trajectory in a space that is connected and 'extended', no longer the benignly authoritative eye.

But this is almost intellectually respectable and rapidly heading toward synthesis, so I return to the 'lodge'. In the 'drift', the 'lodge' can be re-configured (and partly reclaimed, in fact) as a nomadic architecture, a trajectory. The earliest Freemasonic lodges were not (held in) permanent, designated spaces but used meetinghouses and tavern backrooms. The ritual layout of the 'lodge' would be drawn in chalk and obliterated at the end of the meeting. Its emblems were produced like props in a travelling show. What was drawn in chalk was a representation of a historic building – the Temple of Solomon in Jerusalem – but more, it was the representation of a symbolic idea of this building, what Kevin Hetherington, in making an argument for such 'lodges' as spaces of heterotopia, calls 'an expression of the memory of the Temple'.[49] The ambiguity of this 'memory' is well worth playing with, invoking, as it does, not only a personal association and a semi-public memorial, but also an 'art of memory': an esoteric practice in which the visualization of real or imagined architecture serves as a means to commit to memory arcane and highly elaborate dogmatic thought.

The 'drift' adds motion to this: a moving 'lodge' that need not obliterate its traces. Francesco Careri of Stalker has reclaimed the importance of the nomadic for architecture (divorcing the nomadic from sentimentality); each member of the drift becomes a temporary part-pilgrim/ momentary part-refugee disrupted from the *everyday* by 'choice', but able/required to return

Exploring the city as if it were a mountain.
Drifting with children, Exeter, UK (2004).
Photo: Phil Smith.

to the quotidian, by 'choice' at any time, and by 'necessity' eventually. The word 'member' has been chosen firstly because unlike the organized ramble or the guided tour there is no 'consumption' to be had from the 'drift'. It is an action (or improvisation) of production for which organizer/s at most might supply some practical 'toolkit' or structural provocation. Secondly, the 'lodge-like' action of the 'drift' proposes, like Freemasonry, the performance of 'an invented tradition ... symbolized in turning of a stranger into a brother'.[50] The 'drift' obviously has no set ritual for this purpose, but must invent it each time. Some sort of emerging 'geography' and the exchange of détourned 'documentation' (somewhere in between holiday snaps and critical theory) might assist in meeting that task, but would be unlikely to complete it, necessitating some kind of theatrical or performative element in the 'drift'. This turn to performance is, in the context of Freemasonry, a détournement in its turn of Hetherington's account of a move from the secret ritual of the 'lodge' to the bourgeois public space where gentlemen were forced to develop 'a suspension of disbelief in one another as strangers ... done through the reading of signs associated with demeanour, speech patterns and dress codes, in part learned from observing acting at theatres'.[51]

Without ritual and with neither bourgeois 'signs' nor a shared popular radicalism, the 'drift' must improvise its own signs and ritual as it sets its members' ideas and associations in motion in response to the trajectories of the places with which it engages: a rotting fox corpse, half a burned house in small pieces, a confrontation with a manager in a supermarket, a graveyard churned by motorbike tyres and littered with party detritus and torn underwear ... Unlike rambles and tours, where relations are fixed, there are trajectories *within* the 'space' of the 'drifting' group itself, its 'temple' as temporary as chalk, not a container of symbolic walls to be filled with gnosis or agreement. Rather it is *those trajectories themselves*, the changings of the group, that is the space of the 'drift', not in synthesis with a single 'fellowship' or theory but in the explicit playing out of differences, making a 'third space'. According to Bhabha, 'the importance of hybridity is not to be able to trace two original moments from which the third emerges, rather hybridity to me is the "third space" which enables other positions to emerge. This third space displaces the histories that constitute it'.[52]

Crucially, the changings of the drift are not about personal transgression or development, but rather about the diffusion of those identities, their loss of history. The eroticism of the 'drift' is a dispersed one: that is, the eroticizing of space rather than of relations among the drifters. Such unsettling is diffusive in attempting to dissolve the inscriptions on the space of oppressive meanings. To this end Simon Persighetti of Wrights & Sites has developed a whole set of diffusive tactics: the leaving of small figures, tiny wooden villages and dice, chalkings ... diffusions rather than subversions of places, rendering the spaces associative rather than questionable.

Rhetoric

By sixteen I had preached my first Baptist sermon, by seventeen my first Anglican sermon. In my mid-teens I had, with others, wandered the streets of Coventry spreading the gospel. That was in between all the trespass and forced entry, the gleaning of porn, the anatomical investigations in coal bunkers, newts discovered in old pits, Peter Maxwell Davies and Roxy

Music concerts, performing the Babylonian Epic of Creation in a band of ex-Hell's Angels, the touching through and under denim and lace, androgynous displays at cathedral parties, centre-forward in the morning and flanker in the afternoon. Flat green bowls. My teen-years girlfriend was the great-granddaughter of the most famous Baptist preacher ever. The instrumental part of the rhetoric of the *Crab* pieces is their dirty secret: I found something good and I wanted to share it. And that is to be suspected.

The rhetoric of *Crab Walking* is 'Protestant' in character. Its orality, like Protestant rhetoric, is never simply a performance, but a re-performance. It is questionable and yet seeking to speak meaningfully (authoritatively) while suspicious of all (in the case of Protestantism add 'human') voices; it 'always needs more than one voice, it never stops arguing with itself...this is the form its truth claim takes...this absoluteness demands to be represented in the context of a conversation with what it is not'.[53] This is where the practice described here starts, seeking to resolve the question of authority/reality not by a recourse to a first and eternal voice, nor a return to language (logos), but to space.

It follows the disrupted walker Søren Kierkegaard in placing such an intellectual risk as rhetoric *within* the emotional, the associative, the autobiographical. In his book on Protestant rhetoric, Theo Hobson attempts to resolve the contradiction in René Girard's special pleading for a violence resolved by redemptive violence, while admitting that some violence remains, rhetorically, in his model of redemption, in 'the assertion of its overcoming'.[54] In mythogeography there is no claim to a single resolution of this problem of strategy, but a set of inadequate and exponential diffusions into space – perhaps most importantly cinematic-Khlestakovianism, the spatializing of 'character'. It resists premature 'universalisms' and embraces the uncomfortable deferral (as well as the de-historicizing hybridity) of Homi Bhabha's 'third space': 'the notion of a politics which is based on unequal, uneven, multiple and *potentially antagonistic*, political identities'.[55]

The instrumental part of this rhetoric is a kind of shadow of a Gnostic rhetoric as described by Hans Jonas: 'the whole of space...has a malevolently spiritual character, and the "demons" themselves are as much spatial as they are persons. To overcome them is the same thing as to pass through them'.[56] Just as Gnosticism – Christianity's own 'dirty secret' and the motor of much contemporary esoteric activity and narrative weaving – endows 'space' with 'malevolence' so I have sought to endow it with a similar, but amoral energy, a simple performance of itself. 'Place' however is quite different and has all the 365 heavens, un-numbered spaces, mysteries and aeons of fallen matter that any Gnostic nightmare has. It is only spectral patterning – the reduction of these innumerables to a few basic macroscopic patterns – that can 'save' me before I am involuntarily 'born again' in reverse.

The rhetorical aim of the *Crab* project is to give feeling to an idea, to pass on an invitation to explore. The performances were intended to convey the impetus of a journey, the leaps of a dream; the granular texture was intended to provoke the audience's own picaresque reveries. The mixing of science and esoterica, popular culture and seriousness, nostalgia and utopia was a rhetorical device intended as exemplary: as an encouragement to 'drift' (physically and theoretically), to overcome the obstacles (explicitly confronted in *Crab Steps Aside*) and lures of functionalism and passive spectatorship, finding ways to transform these problems into mythogeographical detail.

Velocity
Sexual and postcolonial granularity can freeze the 'drifters' as much as their landscapes. Capital roams, accumulatively, in a way that its subjects cannot. 'Society' has no 'at rest' default mode, no fairness to reference. And like all the other signs in the superfluous landscape, the self is in motion, its geometry easily rumpled by the grit of violence, anxiety or panic. In *Wanderlust*, Rebecca Solnit is appropriately graphic in describing the way that, for women walkers, public places and private parts are crushed against each other. This begs an expansive, spatial, de-centred 'politics of mobility'.

In making *An Exeter Mis-Guide* with Wrights & Sites I was the guest of Exeter Shopmobility, 'an organization helping to provide transport solutions for less mobile people'. Navigating the city with one of its members on motorized wheelchairs we mutually disrupted each other's 'normal' routes. I attempted unwise kerb-leaping, while Colin led me on a convoluted weave around a Georgian 'Hay', lack of dropped kerbs forcing me to examine the pavements and lower walls. I came away with a far subtler understanding of the grains and textures of the city's surface ('You may come to distrust tarmac...') and an unexpected meshing with a different set of exclusions:

> marks, boundaries, lumps and slopes on the city's surface are psychosomatic signs of razing, uprooting and re-laying, the patterns at the very heart of the city bear witness to the borders of a former British minority community living 'at peace, but without mixture; like oil and water in a glass' with a Saxon majority, until ethnically cleansed by 'saint' Athelstan and Edward the Confessor... disruptions that show up in the pavements; tapping at the spines of wheelchair and scooter users.[57]

Vision
On the *Peripheral Vision* drift, we were warned – 'don't get caught up in the deer cull' – and later we found a 'keep out' sign, fallen on its face. Returning it to its silence we walked into the artificial forest, for Moyra Doorly an artificiality that has regenerated an anachronism:

> [T]he Forestry Commission has created something wonderful without realising it. Deep within its plantations lie secret wonderlands where nature spirits have been given a free hand since the trees were planted thirty years ago. Because no one goes there...[58]

Gibson suggests accessing the 'visual field' by fixating on a point; Doorly recommends un-focusing the eyes when looking for fairies. Mythogeographical practice might be to oscillate the techniques, varying the frequency of the oscillation until something, neither physiology nor fairy, resonates.

Similarly, mythogeography's pre-hybridic principle – deferring the synthesis of unlikes – can graft information technology onto archaic esoterica, and vice versa, a cross-breeding that Erik Davis describes in his book *TechGnosis* as implicit in the development of new technology.[59] But there is no place for political credulity, for seeing what we want to. Doreen Massey's modernist metaphorical satellite circling Earth offered materialist means to imagine the motion of social relations about place ('...what gives a place its specificity is not some long internalised history, but the fact that it is constructed out of a particular constellation of relations, articulated together at a particular locus'),[60] contesting the superficial unconventionality of angels by this placing of a technological avatar in the sky. But Massey then dissolves her satellite, outflanking the 'eye' of New Age angelology which is 'beyond' and – unlike the eye in Hindu *Darshana* – only receptive: 'Imagine there is a giant radio station out there in space, beyond the stars, a receiving station, and all you have to do is to beam your thought, your longing to that station'.[61] Not only is binocular vision monocularized here by angelology, but space-time linearized: a 'beyond the stars' wilfully ignorant of a universe receding in all directions.

The point, for mythogeography, is in the suspended relation of the metaphors – satellite, eye, light, array and angel – all part of a drifter's tentative mytho-GPS system. In memetic terms, an element of nostalgia is essential. At these hubs, astronomical access to earlier, simpler memes (sometimes preserved or reconstructed in esoterica) by a kind of ideological red shift is possible. History and pseudo-history are both required for the return of a repressed simplicity. But never the collapse into the welcoming arms of either.

This is the way of *Crab Walking*: not going on a ramble, but taking the ramble on a ramble. It is lazier than a walk with the Ramblers' Association, led by its periphery, making 'strangers' – science and pseudo-science, critical theory and esoterica, movies and theatricality – into 'brothers', de-centredly seeking the opportunity of crisis expeditiously.

Notes

1. Phil Smith is one of the four core members of Wrights & Sites, along with Stephen Hodge, Simon Persighetti and Cathy Turner. For more information about Wrights & Sites, see [online] http://www.mis-guide.com.
2. See *Site-Specific: The Quay Thing Documented, Studies In Theatre and Performance Supplement 5*, August 2000. Also accessible [online] http://www.mis-guide.com/ws/documents/tqt.html.
3. Stephen Graham, *The Gentle Art of Tramping* (London: Ernest Benn, 1929), pp. 38, 17.
4. ibid., p. 51.
5. ibid., pp. 51–52.
6. ibid., p. 220.
7. Geoffrey Murray, *The Gentle Art of Walking* (London: Blackie & Son, 1939), pp. 305–06.
8. Arthur Machen, *Things Near and Far* (London: Martin Secker, 1923), p. 29.
9. Robert Smithson, 'Establishment', in Jack Flam (ed.), *Robert Smithson: The Collected Writings* (Berkeley: University of California Press, 1996), p. 90.
10. Lesley Wade Soule, *The Actor as Anti-Character: Dionysus, the Devil and the Boy Rosalind* (Westport, USA: Greenwood Press, 2000), pp. 28–29.

11. See Susan Blackmore, *The Meme Machine* (Oxford: Oxford University Press, 1999).

12. Margaret Cavendish, *The Blazing World and Other Writings* (London: Penguin, 1994), pp. 183, 189.

13. Gaston Bachelard, *The Poetics of Space* (Boston: Beacon Press, 1969), pp. 113–14.

14. Roger Penrose, *The Large, the Small and the Human Mind* (Cambridge: Cambridge University Press, 2000), pp. 96–97.

15. Paul Nash quoted in James King, *Interior Landscapes: A Life of Paul Nash* (London: Weidenfeld & Nicolson, 1987), p. 1.

16. A tragic carpet was a cloth unrolled for tragic deaths on the eighteenth-century English stage for the purpose of protecting the tragedians' costumes.

17. David Wade, *Li: Dynamic Form in Nature* (New York: Walker & Co, 2003), p. 1.

18. J.A. Scott Kelso, *Dynamic Patterns: The Self-Organisation of Brain and Behaviour* (Cambridge, Mass.: MIT Press, 1997), p. 189–90.

19. ibid., p. 25.

20. ibid., p. 11.

21. Kelso, *Dynamic Patterns*, p. 156.

22. Arthur Machen, *The London Adventure or The Art of Wandering* (London: Martin Secker, 1924), p. 43.

23. Homi Bhabha, *Location of Culture* (London: Routledge, 1994), p. 213.

24. For an explanation of dread space, see Phil Smith, 'Dread, Route and Time: An Autobiographical Walking of Everything Else'; or Phil Smith, 'A Taxonomy on its Toes', *Performance Research*, 11(1), 2006, p. 38.

25. Jeremy Gilbert-Rolfe, *Beauty and the Contemporary Sublime* (New York: Allworth Press, 1999), p. 110.

26. James J. Gibson, *The Senses Considered as Perceptual Systems* (London: George Allen & Unwin, 1968), p. 3.

27. ibid., p. 5.

28. ibid., p. 192.

29. Anthony Freeman, *Consciousness: A Guide to the Debates* (Santa Barbara: ABC-CLIO, Inc., 2003), pp. 60–61.

30. James J. Gibson, *The Perception of the Visual World* (Cambridge, Mass.: The Riverside Press, 1950), pp. 26–27.

31. Professor Clark Barrett, University of California, quoted in *Fortean Times*, 188, October 2004, p. 14.

32. Gibson, *The Perception of the Visual World*, p. 230.

33. 'Positions situationistes sur la circulation', *International Situationiste* (Dec 1959), trans. as 'Situationist Theses on Traffic' in Ken Knabb (trans. and ed.), *Situationist International Anthology* (Berkeley CA: Bureau of Public Secrets, 1981).

34. Kelso, *Dynamic Patterns*, p. 27.

35. Tim Ingold, *The Perception of the Environment: Essays in Livelihood, Dwelling and Skill* (London: Routledge, 2000), pp. 219–20.

36. Bhabha, *Location of Culture*, p. 37.

37. Marion Shoard, 'Edgelands', in Jennifer Jenkins (ed.), *Remaking the Landscape* (London: Profile Books, 2002), p. 140.

38. See Tom Nielsen, 'The Return of the Excessive: Superfluous Places', *Space and Culture*, 5(1), 2002, pp. 53–62.

39. W. Kirk Macnulty, *The Way of the Craftsman* (Hinckley: Central Regalia, 2002), pp. 88, 97, 128.

40. Keith Thomas, *Religion and the Decline of Magic* (London: Harmondsworth, 1973), p. 275.

41. R.J.W. Evans, *Rudolf II and his World* (Oxford: Oxford University Press, 1973), p. 196.

42. Marc Augé, *Non-Places*, trans. John Howe (London: Verso, 1995), p. 92.

43. Doreen Massey points out how economics have neither affected nor explained 'how women's mobility, for instance, is restricted ... "time-space compression" has not been happening for everyone in all spheres of activity'. See Massey, *Place, Space and Gender* (Cambridge: Polity Press, 1994), p. 148.

44. Doreen Massey, *For Space* (London: Sage Publication, 2005), p. 46.

45. ibid., p. 47.

46. David J. Levy, *Hans Jonas: The Integrity of Thinking* (Columbia: University of Missouri Press, 2002), p. 100.

47. Sue Thomas, *Hello World: Travels in Virtuality* (York: Raw Nerve, 2004), pp. 31–37.

48. Tim Ingold, 'Globes and Spheres: The Topology of Environmentalism', in Kay Milton (ed.), *Environmentalism: The View from Anthropology* (London & New York, Routledge, 1993), pp. 31–42.

49. Kevin Hetherington, *The Badlands of Modernity: Heterotopia and Social Ordering* (London & New York: Routledge, 1997), p. 98.

50. ibid., p. 77.

51. ibid., p. 83.

52. Homi Bhabha, 'The Third Space', interview in Jonathon Rutherford (ed.), *Identity: Community, Culture, Difference* (London: Lawrence & Wishart, 1990), p. 211.

53. Theo Hobson, *The Rhetorical Word: Protestant Theology and the Rhetoric of Authority* (Aldershot: Ashgate, 2002), p. 3.

54. ibid., p. 29.

55. Bhabha, 'The Third Space', p. 208. Emphasis in original.

56. Hans Jonas, *The Gnostic Religion: The Message of the Alien God and the Beginning of Christianity* (Boston, Mass: Beacon Press, 1963), pp. 52–53.

57. Wrights & Sites, *An Exeter Mis-Guide* (Exeter: Wrights & Sites, 2003), p. 28.

58. Moyra Doorly, 'Invitation To Elfland', *Fortean Times*, 179, January 2004, p. 42.

59. Erik Davis, *TechGnosis: Myth, Magic and Mysticism in the Age of Information* (London: Serpent's Tail, 1999).

60. Doreen Massey, 'Power-geometry and a Progressive Sense of Place', in Jon Bird et. al. (eds), *Mapping the Futures* (London & New York: Routledge, 1993), p. 66.

61. Sophie Burnham, *The Book of the Angels: Reflections on Angels, Past and Present, and True Stories of How they Touch our Lives* (New York: Ballantine Books, 1990), p. 223.

CRAB STEPS ASIDE

by Phil Smith

First performance: 11 a.m., 27 June 2005 in the Butler Bar, Carlton Theatre, Teignmouth and subsequently a further 23 performances at various venues including The Strode Room, Beaminster; Ness House Hotel, Shaldon; Dawlish Museum; the viewing platform above the Pirates' Chest, Coryton Cove; Old Mill Tea Room, Dawlish; Teignmouth Lido; Old Walled Garden, Mules Park, Teignmouth; Lent Field above Shaldon; and Dawlish Warren Visitors' Centre.

Performer: Phil Smith
Outside eye: Sue Palmer
Map designer: Tony Weaver
Practical support: Julie Owen, Doff Pollard, Celia Hadow, Mike Smith, Andrea Ayres, Mari Sved
Shirt design: Simon Persighetti
Funding and support: Arts Council England, Teignbridge District Council

For help with venues, thanks to: Brenda French of Dawlish Museum, Dawlish Warren Lifesaving Club, Maia for her field, Peter Reynolds (then) of Ness House Hotel and Fiona at the Old Mill Tea Room.

Thanks to fellow 'drifters', of whom there were many more: Stephen Hodge, Cathy Turner, Polly Macpherson, Gill and Derek Greatorex, Fuad Al-Tawil, Helen Chessum, Paul Stebbings, Gemma Conidis, Felicity Cole, Sandra Reeve, Simon Persighetti, Claire Rudkins, Matthew Watkins, Vicky Hemmingway, Eleanor Scott Wilson, Rachel Sved and David Williams.

Phil Smith performing *Crab Steps Aside* (2005). Photo: Derek Frood.

Crab Steps Aside

[Costume: dark blue trousers and a light blue shirt onto which are printed fragments of maps. Light shoes. Props: a small rucksack, a pair of my black boots and a pair of socks. And a small folding stool. Begin by chatting to audience and then sitting on the stool.]

Introduction
I am sitting in a car. In a car park. The rain's falling outside. I don't like this. I'm waiting for the clock to tick round.

This is my own fault. I hate missing things. So I'm always arriving too early. And I don't like arriving by car. Should have caught the train and walked the last bit...

[Check clock on dashboard.]

Just a few minutes.

'Almost time to get the boots on.'

What am I going to say to people? [Look up to the clouds.] If they come...

[Check clock on dashboard.] One minute to go.

And for those 60 seconds I'm sitting, not in the car anymore, not now anymore... I'm in the cockpit of an RAF jet fighter plane and I'm six years old. And there's a man's voice, loud and deep, saying: 'turn on the ignition, turn on the ignition, go on, go on.' And I don't know whether it's a button or a key... and everything is very hard, very cold, everything hurts... the hood of the fighter is falling in on me, the cockpit closing like a fist, everything is beginning to... edge in...

[Break from this. Stand.]

And we step into the drizzle. We put on our waterproofs. I check my camera and notebook. [Do this.] Stephen checks his GPS.

No matter how good you think an idea is when you get it... you never know how it feels until you start to explain it.

And I'm not walking on my own much now, not since my last show, The Crab Walks. In that show I was looking for a bit of myself. This time I'm looking for a bit of everything else. And I want to re-draw the map of it.

[Mime opening a map.]

Because I like maps. Even the dull ones are interesting – they're like bad liars. Because maps are lies really – that's why they're useful – they only tell you what they think you need to know – which is useful to us if we're trying to get somewhere, and useful to those who don't really want us to know everything.

But today, the only map I have is an idea in my head.

[*Upstage, as if to others.*] 'I've said we'll meet outside the pub.'

My dad was a fighter pilot and a rally driver. But I've not sat in the cockpit of a plane since that time when I was six years old. And I only learnt to drive last year.

But I've been trying to fire up that jet for years. To get it to budge, to flex, but there are no wings.

I'm stuck in the metal map of a memory I can't change.

The same encouraging voice. And me still letting my Dad down.

And I think that's why I walk – because I want it to be different this time, I want to understand the things around me, I want the shapes to teach me how to turn on their ignitions … this time, I want to fly.

1: Setting Off

[*As if to those waiting outside the pub.*] 'Hi, hello! Have you come for the walk?'

The pub is – appropriately – the Wild Goose at Combeinteignhead. I first discovered it accidentally on my wanderings for *Crab Walks* … actually, Anjali, who had no idea where she was, she led us to it.

But the people who are gathering now know where they are. 'Hello, Gill! Hello, Derek! There's ten of us, today …' This is the last of three walks I've advertised – one around Dawlish, a night walk in Newton Abbot and now … 'Felicity, hello … Helen, … Fu … Fuad? Fuad. Nice to meet you. This is Stephen, Cathy and Gemma …'

'Well … erm … I'm just going to say a quick word about this strange kind of walking that I do – that's changed my life, not that anyone else has noticed!'

'Ah, hold on, that's Polly … let's wait for her …'

And Polly gets out of the family car and joins us.

[*Walking down towards audience.*]

The last time I had walked with Polly was a couple of weeks before this – we were outside of Dawlish and we came upon a gabion – one of those wire cages packed with rocks. It was in the wall of a private garden. The owner had put too heavy an ornamental stone on top of it and it had bulged its steel braces, like a fat belly hanging over a belt. An example of just the kind of inadvertent fine art that I can rely on Polly to appreciate.

*[*Turning away from audience and then turning back.*]

And garden walls can do that – on another walk, with Claire – we took a book, chose a word at random and then walked until we found it…and then chose another until we found that…and so on…until we came across a garden wall and on it purple flowers in the shape of a revolver, firing purple bullets.[1]

'Good – we're all here now. Quick word before we set off – we're not going to be hiking or rambling, we're going to be "drifting" or – if you want to be posh about it – "dériving". I started doing this kind of walking when a group of us set up an organization called Wrights & Sites.

We started taking people out on exploratory walks. And we soon discovered that we weren't the first group to do this sort of thing – among many others, there'd been a group of artists and revolutionaries, mainly in Paris – called the situationists – in the 1950s and 60s. They went on long walks as kind of rehearsals for changing the world. We stole some ideas from them, and from earlier walkers too…But mostly we tried out our own ideas…we'd walk without having a destination, we'd take things with us to make us see things differently or that would force us to take new routes – we'd leap onto buses without knowing where they were going.

But today's idea – and it may change before we get to that corner there – is 'wormholes'. We're going to be looking for 'wormholes' – now, 'wormholes' are places that take us to somewhere else. Or let somewhere else come flooding in to here. They can be big vistas or tiny little niches.

And one other thing. We're going to walk for four hours; after one hour we'll split the group into two groups of five, after two hours we'll walk in twos and threes and for the last hour we'll all walk on our own. And meet back here at the pub. So, let's go. Which way?'

I'm standing at a junction…dithering…

Wondering if anything will happen.

Wondering if we'll be like Burridan's ass – starving to death between two equally delicious looking carts of hay.

And then we're off!

A goose jacket takes us to China.

Then we're in a brother's Italianate garden.

A lamppost takes some of us to Narnia ... and a meeting with Mister Tumnus ... that piper at the gates of possibility.

Woof! A barking dog wormholes me back to my pram ... and our family dog is attacking me.

Outside a cottage there's a queue of frogs ... 'What's going on in there, then?' The princess is practising!

And someone is reminded of Douglas Bader ...

2: The Green Lane
Very soon a grassy track cuts hard off the metalled road and sharply to our left.

There's an instinctive movement in the group to follow it ... and the moment you feel a thing like that, you have to go with it.

On the green lane, the wormholes continue to open up ...

We come to a gate in one side of the lane ... it has two thick wooden bars ... One is straight and true, the other knobbled and bent.

Gill says: 'The straight one is how you're supposed to live your life, but really it should be the other one.'

And Polly says: 'Actually I could do with one or two things being straight in mine at the moment.'

[*Sit down on stool.*]

You see, Einstein was right – you can't separate space from time.

There are always many different routes, even when you're all on the same path ... And many ways of choosing that path: You can draw a straight line across a map and try to walk it. Or you can take a 'zigzag' walk – take the first right and then the next left and then the next right ... And so on ...

These aren't new ideas – trampers were doing these things a hundred years ago.

Or you can take a theme and try and find examples of it...

Neeow!! Neeow!!

[*React, but stay on the stool.*]

It's a roundabout and in the middle is a clock tower, on the top are winged horses carved in stone and a metal griffon... We're trying to cross over to it, but the problem is you can't see the cars coming round the tower until very late...

OK? Yes? Now!!

And we run! I'm with my friend Matthew... we're looking for angels. We've decided to spend the day in Exeter looking for all traces of angels... and we've got a route – we're going to the four churches dedicated to St Michael and All Angels. And we're on our way to the first when we see the clock tower...

[*Still sitting, hold up hands as if pressed against the surface of the tower, looking up.*]

The white moth, Angel Drift, Exeter, UK (2003). Photo: Phil Smith.

Now we're right up against it...passed it many times, never been this close before...we search its surface for evidence of other winged beings...

'Fear of the Lord is the fountain of life,' says the text above the horse trough. Serpents writhe around the feet of the horses. Bull horns interlock in combat.

Neoooow!! Neeeeow!!

And there it is.

White and cross-shaped on the blood red rock. A white night moth in the grey daylight. Tiny against the thick tower. Our first angel of the day.

Sometimes you don't find what you're looking for – sometimes it's even better.

[*Stand. Take a position, swaying back and forth, as if holding a boat's handrail. This goes into a moment of the 'Billy Dainty dance', a sequence taken from Dainty's imitation of Richard Hearne's 'Mister Pastry' performance in which he sways back, slightly inebriated, before plunging into a few extravagant dance steps and turns. Then back to mime of holding the handrail, swaying.*]

I'm hanging on to the rail on the upper deck of a small ferry boat. Behind us is a leaning storm that has already swallowed the port we left a few minutes ago. Up ahead is the growing island of Herm.

[*Swaying again.*] Whoah!

I'm alone on the upper deck. And I'm feeling as rough as the sea. Paying my dues for last night's bottle of wine after a day's drifting.

[*Breaking from the swaying.*] I'd walked straight out of Guernsey's airport and into the usual strangeness – a pink menhir hidden in the wall of a church. I was alone with the Nazi dummies in the Occupation Museum, I danced a compass onto a beach, and a local man told me the whole island is now run by organized crime. I had tea and a delicious cake called Gacha...

Now I'm making up a Sea Shanty to keep my mind focused and my stomach under control:

[*Sing.*] 'I'm sailing back over the sea...'

It's a terrible song, but I'm not sick.

As we land we all help to unload the stores. Herm is a strange place. You're not allowed to die there. Once you retire you have to leave. Which is odd, as in Celtic times the island was probably reserved for death – a place the Celts brought their corpses for burial.

I pick up a leaf. I've just bought a map of the island from the store.

I take a pen and I trace the shape of the leaf over the map of the island. [*Drawing this in the air.*] The edges of the leaf fit neatly along the coast, and the spine of the leaf almost perfectly matches a road that runs from one end of the island to the other – appropriately called the Spine Road... but the veins of the leaf cut across fields and across all sorts of lines on the map...

[*Walking an edge and down the spine.*]

I set off along the edge of the leaf. Along the beach. I find all sorts of rubbish menhirs – fluorescent light tubes, milk bottles... I stand them up in the sand. A 'menhir' is a standing stone – sometimes shaped like a woman, a lozenge or an egg, the very first things that we humans erected: it's the architecture of the traveller, the nomad, the landmark of the walker. I find a real menhir... well, actually it's a Victorian apology from the islanders for pulling down the original Celtic one and using the bits in stone walls and pavements.

... I drink in the sense of holiness in a scattering of rocks, with every appearance of being the remains of an ancient grave – turns out to be the remains of nineteenth-century quarrying – fine with me – work is holy. And things are never quite what they seem here – when the Nazis made a film here they called it *The Invasion of the Isle of Wight*.

I feel the Pan-ic in the Teazle... a miniature gorse forest that swallows you up... I'm not surprised the island's one-time owner – the novelist Compton Mackenzie – panicked here, spooked by nothing in particular.

I lie in some truly ancient graves.

Panto Valley, Guernsey, drifting simultaneously with Cathy Turner in Bilbao, Simon Persighetti in Manchester and Stephen Hodge in Paris (2004). Photo: Phil Smith.

Walking a vein of the leaf I find a children's den in a wood of bronzely orange trees. I roll over a carpet draped across a barbed wire fence into a field called Panto Valley – and as I do I shout 'He's behind you!' [*Roll across the floor. Then, on knees:*] I'm walking the route of a monastic ghost. A vein takes me through a field full of fairy rings and when I check the map the field is called Fairy Rings.

Then I'm up to my knees in briar … a steep slope, with a teethy sea below, the thorns stick into my shins, I'm treading on fallen furze and I know not what … … bang! A bird of prey goes up right next to me like an explosion! Here the leaf vein is the barbed wire … the only way through is over the wire, and across a field to a gate … can't be that difficult … I balance and … [*Jump*] … fall the field side of the wire … and between me and the gate is only … the biggest bull I have ever seen …

We look at each other –

[*Action: floating in water, dead eyes.*]

My Dad's half-brother's body lies below the waters of Scapa Flow.

His name is in the book in the cenotaph in Coventry – a menhir of sorts …

I'm supposed to be like him – my Uncle Clarrie … Of course, I never knew him – his ship was sunk by a U-boat long before I was born, but we are supposed to have the same sense of the ridiculous.

My Gran told me that he once crawled on his back between the hind legs of a bull until he was staring up into its eyes and said, 'boo'. I may have his sense of humour, but I don't have his courage.

I retrace the vein. [*Back to sitting on stool.*] To Sixpenny Hill, a lane green and curved like a billiard table cush, the kind of bend beyond which you know you will be abducted by fairies. It's too beautiful to be walked.

So I go to the pub and quaff some Patois – four pints of that and you can speak it. Then catch the last boat off the island.

And as it shrinks behind us … I realize I've not really spoken to anyone all day. I've been an apprentice ghost – getting the feel for haunting.

3: The Barrier
Someone's put a barrier across our green lane.

Probably the farmer. It's a small skip, full of rocks and concrete, and above it is a thick wooden pole ...

Whenever you walk you'll always find barriers – walls, barbed wire, just great sheets of wood sometimes, not even trying to be subtle ...

And then there are the invisible ones – tradition, pollution, snobbery, banality ...

Sometimes it feels like the world is being sealed up, branded and nailed down – everywhere the same High Street shop fronts, the same eight logos, everyone wearing the same five labels. And I'm stuck in the metal cockpit and the griffon is saying: 'Turn on the ignition. Go on. Go on.'

But the truth is, the truth is often much better than that. They concrete over one place and another starts to decay interestingly. They put up some building-sized advert, and you know that behind a billboard somewhere else a whole new rainforest is developing.

And Derek is telling me about this quite major road nearby that's been closed and already the grass has begun to take back the macadam. A new green lane is coming into being, just as maybe this one is beginning to die.

[*Into floating in water movement, then into Billy Dainty dance.*]

I like films set in ruined places: on disused piers and derelict dog racing tracks ...

I was walking in Italy, in Tuscany and on top of a hill, and I found this heap of big concrete beams, all higgledy-piggledy, with the wheat growing around them and bubbling up through the middle were red flowers ...

[*I lie down in various directions.*]

... and in the distance [*Holding up the fingers of one hand for the towers*] the famous towers of San Gimignano were all stood to attention ... at right angles to my city of waste. But I was enjoying their randomness just as much as I enjoyed the military planning of that medieval Manhattan on the skyline ...

It's about waste. And knowing *how* to waste.

There's an architect called Tom Nielsen who works in Denmark who talks a lot of sense about this. I'm telling Gill and Derek about his ideas – sparked by the story of the grass growing through the macadam. Or the other way round, I can't remember which now.

Nielsen says we're always going to have waste – the point is *how* we waste. When we build a new housing estate the earth from the foundations gets tipped somewhere else ... kids find it and play on it, grass grows on it and the dog walkers adopt it ... and *that's* how to waste!

We lift up the pole, squeeze under it and around the skip.

In China my friend Paul was stopped at the border between one province and another and told that he did not have the papers necessary to cross over ... the officials demanded something more ... in desperation he offered them the one thing he hadn't yet shown them: his Bubbles Video Shop membership card. The official dutifully wrote down all the details 'Paul Stebbings, Bubbles Video Shop, Radford Road, membership number ...' and then waved him through.

And it's often that moment on a walk, when you cross a barrier, when the walk changes – it stops being a ramble or a constitutional ... it stops being FOR anything ... And it starts to be itself ... it's not following a script anymore ...

'The owners of this land are the cheese people! You watch out! Their men are culling the deer – if they see you – you just run!!'

The woman who's telling us this is very angry – this is on a different drift, now ... around Newton St Cyres. We said 'hello' and we're 'just exploring'. She's walking her dog – she suddenly launches into an attack on the owners of the land. 'She looks down on me! And I've got a degree! They're the cheese people!'

The idea of the drift that day was that we'd keep using our peripheral vision to try to see things we wouldn't normally notice – but I'd kept on forgetting.

We ignore the advice of the woman – 'you'll break your ankles!' – and we take a slightly rough path, but it's fine. And soon we find a wood where we mess about making things. And Cathy, later, says that this calmed her down, after feeling that she was being mis-led by me into the woods with no way through, no proper route ... but I wasn't worried – then ... and soon we found a cool, dark forest of coniferous trees ... with that silence you get ... the whole floor of the forest dead from the darkness and the acidic needles ... except this floor was alive.

I read in a magazine that the endangered species 'fairy' is making a comeback thanks to these artificial forests. For they are artificial – some people believe that these dark forests are our primal forests, where we made our first clearings and erected our first villages ... that's probably a fairy tale ... one of the Grimms. Our primal forests were probably more like country parks; clumps of trees with the ground around them kept clear by herds of grazing deer.

But these artificial forests are bringing back the fairies ...

Apparently to see them you have to un-focus your eyes. [*Make an action of un-focusing my eyes. Then sit down on the stool.*]

When I walk I think of J.J. Gibson.

Gibson was a student of the senses who worked with jet pilots. He believed that we can only really understand sight and touch and smell and hearing as the senses of a body in motion. He studied how the eye and brain take in all the unfolding shapes of the landscape as we move through it – how as one vista folds around us another unfolds in front...

Gibson wrote two famous books... and, just to show what a genius he was, they say completely different things... In the first it's all about how the physical construction of our eye and brain shapes the world in our heads... our perception reaches out into the world, takes it and molds it...

[*Hand action, reaching from brain into the world and molding.*]

In the second book, the shapes that are in the world – the planes of flat lake-beds, the surfaces of motorways, the sides of ravines, the frames of valleys – shape our mind, preparing it to see shapes that recur again and again in the landscape. The world reaches into our mind and molds it.

[*Hand action from the world into the brain, molding action above the head.*]

The mythogeographical way is to believe that he was right both times.

[*Action: swaying on the ship rail, the shorter Dainty dance, the final movement of unfolding the map, un-focused eyes, the leap over the barbed wire fence, sit and do hands raised for close-up to the clock tower, and then, next to my face, I flick open my right hand with the fingers extended.*]

We've been in the woods for three hours now and we still don't know where we are... Cathy is, understandably, getting worried... She wants a marker, a path home. We follow the sound of traffic for about half an hour, but it turns out to be the wind in the treetops. The more we try to find our way... the more lost we feel...

We come into an empty field ringed by tall trees and gun turrets. Plunge into the woods on the other side... Up steep paths that bend and wind... The inner ear swirls... In a green pool... When on the path we find the scattered jaws of some largish predator...

Maybe it's an ABC!! ... an Anomalous Big Cat.

Some people think there are all sorts of big cats – pumas, panthers... even lions and tigers – loose in the English countryside: the beast of Bodmin, the Lion of South Brent... prehistoric survivors, released by private owners or lost by zoos...

But there is another theory – that what we see isn't there ... but WAS. And the imprint is still in our minds. We see some shape: a shadow among the leaves ... and a very old, genetic memory [*Flick open fingers by the side of head*] lights up ...

Of sloping haunches and a long toothed grin, of a loping walk and blazing eyes – a beast that hunted our ancestors ... and then died.

Now – for the first time – I am using my peripheral vision.

4: The First Split and Re-treading the Path

Well. We're one hour into our Wormhole Walk and the green lane splits in two. Five of us go one way. Five the other.

Almost immediately the paths meet again ... and end ... at a gate. Helen is firm that she doesn't want to trespass, so our group re-trace our steps, while the others set off to see if they can find a way through.

I really hate re-tracing my steps. But today I learn to enjoy it. We see so much more on the way back, and things we found before look very different. It's like watching a movie again but from behind the screen.

And when I walk I always have a library of movies in my head. Actually, it's not really a library, it's more like a jerry-built fun park – with the disused pier from *Carnival of Souls* in the Bodega Bay of Alfred Hitchcock's *The Birds* and just back from the seafront there's a nice little park from *Last Year in Marienbad*.

It's not just the films of course ... it's also the places you see them. Strange things always happen to me whenever I go to the Savoy, Exmouth. Although I think that strange things probably happen at the Savoy, Exmouth whether I'm there or not. One day a man woke up, took all his clothes off and tried to climb into *The X Files* movie.

In the 1970s I went to see *O Lucky Man* – a film about corruption in England – and when I came out of the cinema a bloke was being beaten up by a bouncer and the whole thing ignored by a policeman.

I went to a zombie movie where the zombies all moved to shopping mall music. [*Sing a couple of bars of the tune from the shopping mall sequence in* Dawn of the Dead, *'The Gonk' by H. Chappell*] ... when I came out everyone in Coventry was shopping like this ... [*Do the zombie walk – humming the main tune of 'The Gonk'.*]

Whenever I see high cliffs or tall buildings, I expect to see emerging from behind them the Daleks' UFO – from *Daleks, Invasion Earth 2150 AD*. Bernard Cribbins and the Doctor travel forward in time to a ruined and desolate future London, the Tardis materializing just in time to see this Kenwood Chef of a spaceship rising from the pitted towers of the city.

It's a terrible movie and yet that feeling of dread when I first saw it has stayed with me...just the possibility that something awe-ful and impossible could emerge out of a blue sky. It sounds silly, but not to New Yorkers...

UFOs may not be real – but like the ABCs they may be the shape of something that is.

I like dread – and I like dread places, places where you can sense just how big possible is.

I'm standing by a red brick school wall, I'm ten years old, and I've just been rolling my blue plastic toy of Sir Donald Campbell's high speed car Bluebird...and suddenly I feel that I'm not quite part of this world anymore...and that as much as I try I know I will always have to get by with being at least partly separate from it...

5: The Turning Off

It feels like we're getting smaller, just four of us now in our group on the Wormhole Walk... And then there's the time...after a while the senses open wider and wider...letting more things in. The shape of the land, the curve of the bends...even the route itself seems in some way to be *meant*...

It's the kind of feelings you get just before something happens.

I was with my friends Matthew and Vicky – walking from Crediton. We found an old church next to a farmhouse...no other buildings anywhere near. On the church there was no sign, no name, no dedication to a saint...just that feeling. Inside in a trunk were snail-eaten liturgies held at the beginning and end of the Second World War. It was during the Iraq war and the bible on the lectern was open at a passage concerning oil and conflict, and on the yellowing wall was a framed story in italic handwriting...of the consecration of the church and how the church's benefactors left after the ceremony by coach, how on a steep hill the shaft of the coach began to dig into the sides of the horses, how they panicked and at a bend threw out the occupants ...inflicting terrible injuries...but not to one of the passengers – a priest who would go on to serve at the church of St Michael and All Angels that Matthew and I had been heading for on the day we found the angel moth. The priest was thrown high into the air...like an angel...he turned once and landed safely on his feet...[2]

[*Bending forward as if bowing.*]

I'm being closed down by briars...The thorns dig in and hold me back...'Where's Phil gone?'

This *was* a path once...Up ahead there's a light through the thorns...The others join me...We find a blue plastic rocket...And turn back...

One of those moments when you think things are just about to take off...

But, no ...

And we're falling backwards up the rabbit hole ...

Things speed up ...

We're in a cave – it's flooding! Having to dive under the water ... to get out ... [*Gasp.*] The drawing and holding of breath ... the cold on the face ...

We're hostages – trapped in a box, strapped to the bottom of a racing lorry ... the rumble of the shaft ... the heat in the box rising ...

Falling and slipping ... nothing to get hold of ... A stick stabbed into the slope ... We're all sliding on the steep mud ... To the bottom of the incline ... and we stumble out onto the path – and breathe again.

And Fuad is explaining what a Ziggurat is: a labyrinthine spiral reaching up to heaven.

Just as we have spiralled back down to earth.

And we all note how that enclosed, spiky space up there had shaped how we were talking. It had all been about bodies, caves, hostages, and now as the canopy of trees opens up to the sky we talk about psychotherapy and heaven. The places we choose to be in change how we feel.

[*Taking chair close to audience, sit down.*]

It's dark and shadowy and the air is thick with the richness of a deep beer. I'm in a pub in the city of O and the man opposite me is someone who's been both a colleague and an employer for a number of years and he has my attention – he's talking about war rooms. His old college pal is someone big in American politics. Used to be in the ONI, Office of Naval Intelligence – part of the US secret service – my interest is becoming reluctantly real.

In this pub in the city of O, this man is telling me about the appearance of, the location of, and events in the United States War Room during the Iraq Conflict. He describes a circular room. Its curved walls filled with TV screens. And from it, corridors branch off to other rooms from where messengers and advisers rush back and forth.

We don't leave the pub table, but I feel like he's leading me down these corridors – second hand to him and third to me. And all the more convincing for being so. After all, you wouldn't believe someone in a pub who told you they were actually there!

And what a place this man in the city of O is describing – a room where you can be a couch potato and the ruler of the world at the same time!! When – mayhem! – on one of the screens a US Army officer is clambering up a statue of Saddam Hussein – yes, THAT statue of Saddam Hussein – the one the TV chiefs have chosen to symbolize the sort of home-grown overthrow of Saddam that the US so desperately wants to present to the world – and now this joker of an army officer is climbing up it with a Stars and Stripes! 'Get that goddam thing off of there!!' It echoes down the corridors, across the screens, along the fibre optics, bouncing off the satellites. It's democracy. The word is spoken in the War Room and in a Baghdad square the Iraqi flag replaces the Stars and Stripes.

There's a secret map ... it spreads under the skin and through the air we breathe. It pierces every cloud in every sunset ... sometimes you're smuggled a little piece of it ... and sometimes you only step off the pavement and you're 'invited' to change that decision.

Parts of the B2 bomber are made in every state of the USA – not because it's cheaper or more efficient that way, but because the B2 bomber is part of what binds that country together.

You can learn French, you can study quantum mechanics, maybe you can recite lists of kings and queens – but it you don't know geography then you don't know the world.

We drink up in that bar in the city of O. And still I don't really know.

[*Mime placing empty pint glass on table.*]

Everyone has maps like that. Partly something we've been told about, partly something we've seen or read about.

Every Sunday I went to see my Gran and we passed this little factory, where it turned out they made the Iraqi super gun and were all working for MI6.

Wherever you look you'll find wonders:

Eleanor found a pair of plastic breasts on Mamhead Hill.

On a drift in Paignton with my daughter Rachel we came across a lonely garage sale, where we bought a music box – the motor is broken and it only plays about one note a day – the whole tune will take months – but at night, I can be putting out my children's school uniforms for the morning, and it plays its note and suddenly I'm in a bigger map of time.

In the Rue de Les Morts Cemetery on Guernsey I found a card stuck behind the wood of the noticeboard ... it read: 'One day we will find out what *really* happened on that dreadful night.'

On the Cote de Granite Rose near Ploumana'ch I turned a corner and there was a twenty-foot high accidental sculpture of the head of an alien grey.

In a housing estate in Munich I lifted my camera to take a picture of the first *red* squirrel I had seen in 30 years and realized that I had it loaded with black and white film.

Walking down the valley from the Mad Monk's Chapel we trespassed through a deserted farmyard where a barnful of sheep were listening to 50s swing music.

And maybe one day I'll find the Strategic Reserve...

In the Second World War a bureaucrat was asked to draw up a list of the steam locomotives the army might use in the event of a German invasion. Of course the invasion never came, the locomotives were never assembled, but the list remained, and it was found by a railway enthusiast and the story went around of a huge, secret collection of steam trains, somewhere in England, probably underground...waiting for a national emergency...their furnaces burning.

Of course, it doesn't exist. I don't think.

Along what railway lines do ideas run?

What's behind that curtain?

What's all this steam?

6: Munich

[Action: *trying to part steam with hands.*]

I don't recognize these corridors...I have to get back to my locker!

I'm in the Volksbad in Munich. And...um...I'm not wearing any clothes at the moment.

Where the bloody hell am I? Follow your instincts!

Ahah! What's behind this door?

[Mime *opening door. Then action: the Bill Dainty dance, into the roll into Panto Valley, stand and reach hand above head and 'mold brain' with fingers, then into underwater floating with dead eyes.*}

I'm on a walk in Munich with Paul...We'd begun at a huge building that turned out to be the gateway to a cemetery. We tried all the doors, and one opened, into a long marble corridor. On one side, behind glass screens, were rows of coffins.

One of the screens has grey curtains drawn across it...there's something final about that grey. Maybe we're not supposed to be in here?

Cemetery in Munich, drifting (2004). Photo: Phil Smith.

Paul opens the door at the end of the corridor and white light streams in as if from heaven... Blinded, we stagger outside, where a cruciform sign points to Krematorium in one direction and in the other to Toiletten...

It's starting to get dark when we arrive at the Volksbad – [*using hands to part steam*] – it's the 'people's baths' – once inside the bathing area complete nakedness is the rule. So I leave my boots and things in a locker [*gesturing upstage to my boots and rucksack*] and set off into the honeycomb of corridors and steam. I enter a room of dry heat, but I miss my footing and end up on the hot slabs – ah, ah, ah, ah!!

[*Dancing about on the hot slabs – into action of Billy Dainty dance reaching hand over hand over hand, on the spot, then break from this.*]

... I dash into the cold pool at the centre of all the corridors – ooh! [*Relief.*]

But it's a sort of naked version of the war room arrangement. And when I've had enough I wander back through the corridors. But I don't recognize these corridors. I have to get back to my locker. O, where the bloody hell am I? Use your instincts!

Ahah! What's behind this door?

[*Mime opening the door – now halfway upstage, left – and walking out.*]

...and I emerge, steaming and naked, into the café! – where, of course, everyone is completely clothed. I back off and disappear into the corridors of steam.

[*Sit on the stool, upstage.*]

But even naked in a Bavarian café, there is no such thing as a wrong turning.

In San Gimignano, with my daughter, Rachel, we tried to walk the city in a spiral and the city wouldn't let us – but even so, in a side street we found a lonely, sinister collection of stuffed birds.

In Prangins, on the shore of Lake Geneva, I approached the door of a chapel, pinned to it was a piece of paper that read: 'séance'. I didn't mean to go in, but as I leaned to look through the keyhole it opened with a click. [*Make click. Illustrate the door with hands.*] No one was there. I stepped back and it closed. [*Illustrate the door with hands. Make click.*]

Just a month ago David and I set off into a hot London afternoon...we stopped at a small, quiet café for some coffee and water...I asked to use the toilet and was directed through doors almost off their hinges, down a stumble of crumbling steps and into a ruin of a courtyard, where looking up, there, framed in a square map...

The mist comes down over Combeinteignhead...As thick as the steam in the Munich baths.

7: Last Hour

I've parted from Helen now and I'll be walking on my own for the last hour of our Wormhole Walk. [*Walking on the spot, fast.*] But I'm determined to find this No Man's Land Helen has told me about. I don't normally walk this fast, but I'm seeing every detail even at double speed. A copse looms out of the curtain. The signs of children's play things do nothing to take away its feeling of...dread. Just a few trees and yet I'm feeling for the first time a hint of that real panic that I've often written about...I try to distract it by hurrying on...

But things don't have to always be good...there doesn't have to always be a happy ending!

In a cave under Langstone Rock...I found a big crab shell...When I picked it up it flapped like a piece of soft flesh...

At the end of the last show I explained how I had come to realize that the empty crab shells I'd found were not victims of herring gulls, but the discarded costumes of crabs that had grown into new, bigger, hardening selves...

...but this shell was soft, this crab had never had the chance to harden into a new self.

I force myself to stop and look into the trees. Not to stop the uneasiness, but to try to begin to enjoy it.

Up ahead the mist clears for a few yards and I come out into the unprepossessing junction of No Man's Land. But I'm not happy here and my anxiety takes a material form – a tulpa – an unreal dog like that dog of my Pop's that crawled into my pram and bared its teeth.

We stare across the meaningless junction at each other – me, frozen, him at attention beside a rusted stock-car wreck … his owner appears and I pretend to be at ease …

'Is this No Man's Land?'

He says something about the rugby international and I realize I haven't been in television time for quite a while now …

I say something, but I'm not listening to myself, I'm looking at the blast of shotgun pellets in the side of the car wreck … in my head I'm in the badlands … film noir USA … But in a faint colour print.

We talk to each other as if we're mouthing words underwater … I hear myself asking for directions – I never ask for directions!! But I only hear the first of his replies and I stagger off at speed.

[*Sit down on stool.*]

I'm tired now. Worried about not getting back to the pub in time to meet everyone.

The mists swallow me again. I'm walking through lace curtains. Out of the veil emerge subtly rounded, voluptuous hills, green velvet under a frosting of sugar … soft and fragile. And beneath it, the brown and grey of the grave comes winking through at me … batting its big eyes, opening its huge mouth … A smile stretching hundreds of yards of stone wall … and I'm not stopping now … I'm not scared … I'm loving this … the hard cockpit all around me is starting to unfreeze … the cold metal warms even in the afternoon cold … and I begin to really move … to fly …

As the once-abducted pilot shouts at the end of *Independence Day* as he flies his jet fighter into the heart of a UFO the size of a city: 'Hello boys, I'm back.' And I'm not standing by the school wall anymore.

All those people I've walked with … they are the power that lifts not me, but unseen eyes that float out of my head, angels measuring the land stretched like a canvas … their wings like compasses, the fields like a wonky chequerboard.

And my Dad walks now … no more Vampire jets or rally cars …

And despite one of them falling dead on one of their walks, my Dad and his friends continue their epic journeys. A soldier on exercise was amazed to find these white-haired men striding for the top of Snowden.

And he powers me now...

[Get up from stool.]

I'm hovering like a jump jet...above myself...watching my every step...unrolling a map I've been preparing earlier...

The beach hut begins to break up in the waves.

[Pointing out places as if on a map on the floor.]

Dread places, Z worlds, accidental museums, wormholes, soft places, superfluous places...All the pieces are spreading...

[Action sequence: Handrail swaying, Billy Dainty dance, unfolding map, un-focusing eyes, hands up on the clocktower gesture, fingers snap up by the side of the face and then into hand over hand over hand action, ending as if grasping a door handle.]

Ahah! What's behind this door?

[Mime opening door. Through it and walking very fast.]

And I walk out onto the map.

*[Action: Catch my breath. Sit down on stool.]

During the war my Mum lived for a while on a farm. At harvest time she would help to beat the last square of corn left standing at the centre of a field...Clap! Clap! Clap! Until the rabbits ran from the last few stalks...Bang! Bang! Bang!

I see the geometry of that square from the inside.

I imagine the dance of it.[3]

[Into Billy Dainty dance, end with a flourish.]

I loved Billy Dainty. He was my favourite of all the pantomine performers I met: Mister Pastry – he gave me a golly – Frankie Howerd – 'Sit on the stooooool!' Hope and Keen, Janie Marsden – she gave me a kiss – Nat Jackley with his elastic neck ... but Billy Dainty was my favourite. He was a comedy dancer – and he moved to the trombone with a deep, heavenly kind of grace.

There was something beautiful inside his send-up. Like you could only do that if you had some secret, or you'd signed some pact with the angels of Pantoland. Or the devils.

[*Extended sequence of Billy Dainty's 'Mister Pastry' dance.*]

My friend Paul's dad was theatre doctor in Nottingham, when Billy called him in. Billy's calf was swollen with a thrombosis – it was playing a blood trombone in his veins. But Billy refused to cancel his act that night – and so he danced for the last time. It was a dance of death and Billy died quietly, in bed, a few weeks later.

Billy once took a bow at the end of his act and his toupee fell off... he said: 'O well, you might as well know it all...' and took out his teeth.

[*Sit down on the stool.*]

He reminds me of my Pop – my grandfather – every night, he'd wrap up his calves in bandages. He'd be in his big blue armchair, where he always sat and where, one night, he was struck by a sudden, terrible pain – a thrombosis – and died, while I was far away.

[*Pull up my trouser legs as if to wrap my legs in bandages.*]

Sometimes I feel that my walking is a dance of death.

In the cellar of the Well House pub in Exeter's Cathedral Yard – what I think of as the mythogeographical heart of all this nonsense – is a case and inside is what seems to be a skeleton. Actually, it's two skeletons, jumbled, male and female – which is interesting because long before the archaeological pathologist made this discovery, there's always been a story of a besotted nun and monk who together threw themselves down a well in the Cathedral Yard. The important thing though is the text above the case of jumbled bones. It says: 'Birth is the first step unto death.'

[*Take off shoes and socks, rub calves.*]

These days I get these pains in my calves. They seem to go away when I'm walking. As if my walking is keeping me alive. And if I was ever to stop... I might be struck with a sudden, terrible pain – in my red armchair. And, maybe, get the chance for one last dance of death.

[*Hum the mall music from Dawn of the Dead – 'The Gonk' – as I put on the socks and walking boots. Probably tie one boot and then end music. Carry on putting on other sock and boot. Stay sitting.*]

Of course, that's a lot of nonsense... the pains don't have anything to do with thromboses or death or anything of the sort. They're most likely a legacy of the race walking I did as a youngster.

The misty hills above Combeinteignhead, UK. Wormhole Walk (2004). Photo: Phil Smith.

I once made the back page of the *Coventry Evening Telegraph* for being disqualified for running in a walking race. It was the city championships and I was the reigning champion. I always used the same tactic: stick on the shoulder of the leader and then accelerate to the line with 400 yards to go ... it was a sublime experience – to be exhausted and yet to go to the next level.

But in one of the league races that summer a new lad had set off at a tremendous pace and I couldn't keep up with him and I'd had to drop out.

Come the day of the championships, I was determined not to get left behind. Again we set off at a blistering pace, but this time I kept with him. With 400 yards to go I was still on his shoulder and as the bell went for the last lap I deployed my usual tactic ... bad move ... 200 yards later my legs had gone and I was all over the track, and up ahead I saw this judge waving me off – it's a technical offence – called 'lifting' – my feet were coming up off the track. I wasn't sprinting or anything, but I was disqualified – and I turned round and they were waving off my rival as well – and then the next two walkers ... all disqualified ...

And it hurt – and it was disappointing ... but for those 200 yards when the four of us were really going for it – that was beyond athletics ... that was metaphysics ... that was alchemy ... that was flying.

I'm back at the pub now. I can see myself as a little counter on a map of Combeinteignhead.

For one day the map *is* the territory.

Phil Smith performing *Crab Steps Aside*, Dawlish (2005).

And the little boy *is* the pilot.

[*Get up and pack the shoes and socks into the rucksack. Then fold up the stool and pack that in the rucksack. Zip up the rucksack.*]

In the pub, there are stories of an argument with a farmer, of watching a woman clean a church, of old books, apples and a story on a wall, of a smell of washing and of India.

And later, of a Christmas tree that took Fuad back to happy times in Iraq.

[*Slinging the rucksack over one shoulder.*]

Outside the pub, on the road, are two patches of spilled petrol glowing like eyes – or like the roundels on the wings of an RAF plane.

Notes
1. Passage from asterisk on was eventually removed for the performances.
2. This paragraph was eventually removed for the performances.
3. Section from asterisk eventually removed for the performances.

PART 3: DEE HEDDON

TREE: A STUDIO PERFORMANCE

by Deirdre Heddon, Dorinda Hulton, Helen Chadwick, Arianna Economou and Horst Weierstall

Performer: Dee Heddon
Dramaturge and Director: Dorinda Hulton
Choreographer and Director: Arianna Economou
Composer: Helen Chadwick
Installation Artist: Horst Weierstall
Sound Designer: Duncan Chave
Video Documenter: Peter Hulton

Duration: 30 minutes

Tree was performed at the Performance Studio, School of Performance Arts, University of Exeter, July 2003.

One Square Foot, from which it developed, was a co-production between Theatre Alibi, echo-arts Cyprus and the School of Performance Arts, University of Exeter. It was funded by Arts Council South West, the AHRB (Arts & Humanities Research Board), Devon County Council, and Exeter City Council.

Photographs © Juanita Gill, Horst Weierstall and Dee Heddon.

Tree: A Studio Performance

[A large circle of mismatched wooden chairs fills one part of the studio. The circle itself has been filled with lots of dried leaves, of all different colours and sizes, collected from the grounds of Exeter University's Thomas Hall during the week. They are therefore taken from many different trees planted in the landscaped gardens, and close to where Big Tree, the Sequoia, is located.

SFX: leaves rustling in the wind, and the sound of birds, recorded at the site of Big Tree.

The circumference of the circle is punctuated by a number of different 'objects'. At one point, there is a large charcoal etching on white paper attached to the wall – it is a sort of figurative drawing of a tree – but not easily or immediately identifiable as such. Leaning against this is one long, large, straight branch. I stand at the door and greet everyone as they come into the studio, and then wait for them to sit in the circle. I then walk to the circle and stand in front of the large charcoal etching.]

This is my square foot.

[I bend down and place four pine cones, taken from Big Tree, on the floor, as if marking the corners of a square. Once I have done this, I step into the square foot, and walk through it, into the centre of the circle. I then lie on my back, on the floor, in the centre.]

I lie on my back, on the floor, in the centre.

I lie, looking up. My head feels supported. I'm unlikely to fall off the earth. Above me, the trees make a circle. And in the centre a white empty space. This space is cut up by flight paths. Black birds, high up. Lower down, smaller breeds. Finches, maybe? I should know. I *should* know. Beyond the frame, the sound of a train. A long-distance runner. The Penzance to Glasgow perhaps? My route home.

The crown of the tree sways. Scots Pine? Montreal Pine? I should know. *I should* know. Douglas Spruce, Fir, Willow, Ash, Oak, Rowan, Hazel, Elm, Maple, Sycamore, Juniper, Beech, Silver Birch, Redwood. Wellingtonia. Big Tree. Sequoia. [*Long call.*] SEQUOIA.

[*I sit up and return to the place of the etching and sit on a small wooden bench there, as if sitting under Big Tree.*]

This tree, the Redwood, the Wellingtonia, the Big Tree, is called Sequoia. Dedicated to the Indian Cherokee who was called Sequoiah. Sequoiah was the last man to have single-handedly devised an alphabet. It took him twelve years, but in 1821 Sequoiah had finally completed the alphabet of the Cherokee language – a total of 85 symbols.

[*I stand up and draw an imaginary letter in the air.*]

1838. It was the winter of 1838. That's important. At that time, the Cherokee Indians were living on their own land, in what is now called Georgia, USA. And then all 20,000 of them were forcibly removed, and made to walk West, all the way to Oklahoma. The white man wanted their land; alongside the gold that had recently been discovered on it. As they walked, they died; 4,000 of them – from cold and starvation.

[*I bend down and pick up three of the cones that have marked the square. I put them in my pocket, leaving one cone to mark this spot. Once I have done this, I walk very slowly around a quarter of the circle, accompanied by the sound of a low rumbling, which continues throughout the following section. This is, in fact, the sound of a chainsaw cutting a tree, played back very slowly. I stop at the quarter circle mark.*]

That walk would be known as the Trail of Tears. Where mothers' tears fell, white roses grew. White roses continue to mark the trail of tears today. 1814.

It was the winter of 1814. At that time, the crofters of Strathnaven, Scotland, were minding their land. And then the orders came and the enforced evictions began. Houses were burnt, possessions destroyed, tenants turfed out. People died of cold and starvation. This was the beginning of the Highland clearances. In 40 years, 40,000 people were cleared from the Isle of Skye alone. Many of those people from the Highlands emigrated to the 'new worlds' including Canada and America.

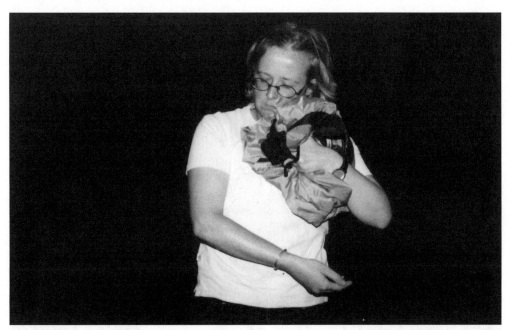

I begin to slowly remove my jacket, crumpling it into a bundle which I caress and cradle as I turn in a small circle.

[*I put my hand in my jacket pocket and remove white feathers, all collected from the grounds of Big Tree. I let these drop from my hands, and form a bundle in the circle. I then step into the circle and again draw an imaginary large letter, D, in the air. I begin to slowly remove my jacket, crumpling it into a bundle which I caress and cradle as I turn in a small circle. This is executed very slowly and eventually I place it carefully on top of the pillow of feathers. This might be a small child, killed from the deprivations suffered on the Trail of Tears. In fact, the shape I am making as I cradle my jacket is an 'e'. I slowly remove a second cone from my pocket and leave it next to the bundle. The rumbling sound has now increased in volume.*

Once the cone has been placed, the sound changes dramatically and without warning. It sounds like an electronic voice, and in fact it is my voice speeded up beyond recognition. As I walk around half the circle, the speed slows down so that eventually you can hear what is actually being said, 'Cutting trees I never saw him plant', at which moment the sound stops suddenly. By this time, I am at the next designated point in the circle, marked by a wood cutting trestle and a very small pine sapling planted in a shoe – in fact, my shoe. I take the third cone out of my pocket and hold it for the audience to see.]

Big Tree.

[*I place the cone on the floor next to the planted tree and look at it.*]

Little tree. There's no comparison.

Dee Heddon performing *Tree: A Studio Performance*.

[*I sit down on the trestle.*]

Each letter in the Gaelic alphabet is the start of a name of a tree. I read somewhere that children in Scotland used to be taught their alphabet by listing trees rather than letters. A = Ailm, Elm; B = Beith, Birch; C = Coll, Hazel; D = Darrach, Oak; S = [*I draw an S in the air*] Seileach, Stewart; A = [*I draw an A in the air*] Ailm, Andrew; D [*I draw a D in the air*] = Darrach, Dee.

My brothers and me. We'd pile into the green and white Forestry Commission Land Rover. My brothers and me in the back. We'd sit on the hump over the wheel. Hard metal. And with every bump in the road we'd go flying up in to the air, and then down again, hard, with a bang, until we reached the middle of the forest.

M – [*Draw M in the air*] Muin, Mother, my mum was at home.

F – [*Draw F in the air*] Fearn, Father.

My dad was a forester. He'd spend a minute surveying the scene. I'm not sure what he was looking at – the heights, the distances in-between, the surrounding spaces? Once he'd found the right tree, he'd stand us at a distance from it, and then start up the chainsaw.

At a precise point in the operation, the tree would begin to move a little. And then as he cut through the last hinge, the mighty shout that we'd all been waiting for would finally come: 'TIMBER!' Then the tree would come falling through the air, crashing through its neighbours, landing with a bounce on the ground below, dust, sawdust, and a big empty space where the tree used to be. The sound, the smell. Pine. Clean. Fresh. The meat of the tree.

[*Sound of a vocal chant – almost resembles a cross between a Gaelic lament and a Native American song. I stand up and walk into the centre of the circle, and this time lie on my front.*]

Dried mud, fibrous bark, dried leaves, tufts of grass, shiny carcasses of deceased insects, stones, moss, fragments of wood, half an acorn, a fly that lands for a rest, [*I get to my knees*] my breath, moving everything continuously.

[*Using movement and gesture only I repeat the contents of the square foot – everything that I observed in the square foot when I looked at it closely – gradually coming to stand again. The recorded vocal lament continues throughout. At the end of this movement sequence, I begin to walk around the circle again. This time, I not only walk the circumference, but then begin to walk a smaller circle inside the large circle, and then an even smaller circle, which will eventually bring me to a position opposite the one in which I started. This configuration resembles the actual site, where the small sapling tree faced the Big Tree.*]

Tufts of grass.

A soundtrack accompanies my walking; it is composed of a score that accompanies me speaking. This recorded text is not rehearsed text – it is simply a recording of what I first told composer, Helen Chadwick, about my square foot. The words of this soundtrack are: 'It's partly about moving I suppose, it's kind of again about that rooting and moving, whether one can be rooted and move?' The question, 'whether one can be rooted and move?' is repeated throughout the duration of my walking.

Marking this last place on my circling journey is a small square of grass, itself set inside a square wooden frame. On top of this are some leaves.]

In Virginia, there's a small town called Glasgow. In Kentucky, there's a small town called Glasgow. In Montana, there's a small town called Glasgow. I left Glasgow in 1998, and moved to Exeter. That was my decision to make. [*Written phonetically*] Ni-Ka-na-uay-ku-na-na-hna-i. Safe place. Cherokee. Sequoiah never learnt any English, but he had witnessed people reading and writing and had seen what he called 'Talking Leaves'. And he wanted that opportunity for his own people. Sequoiah's alphabet is his testimony. The leaves began to talk Cherokee and they continue to do so. [*Written phonetically*] Hahna. My safe place. Gaelic. I leave you a talking leaf.

[I pick up the square of grass and walk around the circle, passing out leaves to audience members. Each leaf is inscribed with a word from the text. As I walk, I sing a song composed during my improvisation sessions with Helen Chadwick:

You can find or make a route,
my story in your story.
Your life is not yours alone.
You can find or make a route,
your story in my story.
You can be here and there.
You can find or make a route,
my story in your story.
One person's present
is perhaps someone else's theft.
You can find, or make a route,
your story in my story.
The frame is always porous.
You can find or make a route,
my story in your story.
Your story in my story.

When I get back to where I started the song, I replace the square of grass and take the final cone from my pocket to mark this final spot. I've travelled a long way.]

ONE SQUARE FOOT: THOUSANDS OF ROUTES[1]

Deirdre Heddon

Choose a square foot in Exeter that has some personal significance for you.

Dorinda Hulton

The myth of autobiography is
that the story is singularly formative,
that the gesture is coherent and monologic,
that the subject is articulate and the story articulable, and
that the narrative lies there waiting to be spoken. (Smith and Watson, 1996)[2]

Pre-Amble

As I attempt to reflect upon both the process and outcomes of *One Square Foot: tree*, at least in relation to my part in it, I am reminded of Cathy Turner's warning that 'there is an uneasy relationship between performance practice and its analysis'.[3] This is most keenly felt when that analysis is undertaken by the practitioner, post-performance. As Turner admits, 'that sequence of trial and error, choice and chance, intention and recognition is unlikely to unfold in a linear, logical and coherent fashion'.[4] At the outset, in writing this self-reflective contribution to *Walking, Writing and Performance* I must acknowledge that *One Square Foot: tree* was devised in July 2003. I am therefore returning to it some years after the event. In that time, a lot has happened. Not least, I have moved away from Exeter and returned 'home'. The train journey from Penzance to Glasgow is now remembered rather than experienced, and there is a huge difference between one and the other. In the intervening period, I have also picked up other books and articles (I am

particularly indebted to geographer Doreen Massey's ideas about space), engaged in other conversations (with Carl and Phil, to name just two) and encountered other performances (including *The Crab Walks* and NVA's midnight mountain walk, *The Storr* in 2005).

Some of these new encounters have enabled connections with ideas already at work in my mind (and body) at the time of *One Square Foot: tree*; some extend those, some challenge them and some enable me to 'read' my own work as if with the benefit of someone else's hindsight: 'Ah-hah, so *that's* what I was doing'. I am entirely grateful for the time between then and now. As Mike Pearson insists, the documentation of a performance can only ever be another, different, performance.[5] It feels like a privilege to be able to revisit *One Square Foot: tree* and to perform it anew. Rather than pretend or impose a linearity or logicality or coherency on the process of devising *One Square Foot: tree*, this reflection is intended to mirror the process of structure and chance, the intentionally guided and the fortuitously accidental. In the spirit of the project, the voices of my collaborators appear alongside mine.

Setting Off

Stories related to the past: *i) Using the first person ('I') tell the 'story' of a personal memory associated in any way with your square foot. ii) Using the first person ('we') tell the 'story' of a personal memory associated in any way with your square foot. iii) Using the second person ('you') tell someone who is not present, but who comes to mind when you think of your square foot, something you remember about them. iv) Using the third person ('he' or 'she') tell the 'story' of something that has happened to someone else associated with your square foot. v) Using the third person ('they') tell the 'story' of something that has happened to someone else associated with your square foot. [...]*

As ever, with every good wish, Dorinda.[6]

I have been working (researching and practising) in the field of autobiographical performance for a number of years now. In this time of mass-mediated confession, the use of personal material in performance seems both persistently timely but also challenging, precisely because of the ubiquity of the confessional mode. I consider the roots of autobiographical performance to lie in women's radical performance practice of the late 1960s and early 1970s, which issued explicit challenges to the minimalist and formalist trends dominating the art world, but also to the misplaced notion of art as being neutral and in some way 'unlocated' (ungendered, unsexed, unraced, etc.). The autobiographically informed work that erupted into visibility primarily as a result of the second-wave feminist movement was undoubtedly connected to that well-turned phrase, 'the personal is the political'.[7] I admire this early work – its passion, bravery and deep necessity. However, confronted as I am in the early twenty-first century by the glut of personal moments made public, across all forms of media, I am often reminded of Geraldine Harris's sharp insight that 'not all of the personal is political in *exactly the same way* and to the same effect'.[8] As a teacher of autobiographical performance practice, I am also aware that not all of the personal, within the realm of performance, is necessarily interesting. Just because something is drawn from 'real life' does not make it intrinsically more engaging than any other material.

In the end, lived experience is simply another resource, material to be used, transformed, reinvented; and the 'success' of that will depend on the skill of the performer and their craft at turning the material into a performance, where the work is being made for a spectator. In this, I am reminded of Lisa Kron's witty perspective: 'The difference between [performance and] therapy is that therapy happens to you, performance happens to the audience. It's not about you reliving this, it's about you letting the audience do it'.[9] I would also argue that, when successful, the fact that the material *is* drawn from real life *does* make a difference; arguably, the matter of lived experience matters.

In entering into the realm of autobiographical performance, I am only too well aware of the criticisms frequently made of the form, typically coalescing around notions of solipsism:

Many artists draw all their resources from themselves and continually reflect only their own image.[10]

The dangers in autobiographical art are legion: solipsisms that interest an audience of one.[11]

It was, then, something of a relief that in *One Square Foot*, the skill to be harnessed was not mine alone but a whole team of creative practitioners: Dorinda Hulton (project initiator, dramaturge, and director), Arianna Economou (choreographer and director), Horst Weierstall (installation artist), and Helen Chadwick (composer). Moreover, though I was the initial catalyst for the stories generated around a square foot selected by me, working with a team of artists inevitably led to a process of both narrative and aesthetic symbiosis. Just as their artistic specialisms enabled different engagements with the site and different modes of working with the material, so their unique perspectives on the square foot merged with and adapted my own.

Professor J. Anderson (Consultant Ecologist for *One Square Foot*):[12]

[*Exploring my chosen 'square foot'*] We can see this is from under a conifer. The characteristics of a conifer are they produce fragments of litter and bark that break down very slowly. And these produce soils which are always very rich in organic matter. They decompose very slowly and therefore much of the nutrients are being released very, very gradually from this material. And this is why the roots are all in here, picking up the nutrients and the fascinating thing about these roots [...] is that [they] have an association with fungi [...]. There is a symbiosis, which means that both partners gain from this association.

One Square Foot, in its entirety, was a collaborative process. I apologize in advance to my co-creators for any misrepresentation of the process and of their part in it; the memories here are wholly mine, and like all memories this account is both filled with unconscious and conscious revisions and inventions, and riddled with holes. Translating creative practice into written text also necessitates a wilful act of creativity.

Ground Plans

Record the ambient sound at the site of your one square foot.
Record any other sound in some way related to the themes of your one square foot.
Post the recordings to me with any written commentary/explanation you want to add.

Best wishes
Helen

The *One Square Foot* project was a practical research enterprise initiated and managed by Dorinda Hulton, a professional director and part-time lecturer at the University of Exeter Drama Department. Hulton has long been interested in the role of the actor in creating performance, developing models that facilitate the performer's creative practice.[13] For Hulton, a primary aim of *One Square Foot* was to explore the impact of different creative methodologies on the actor's craft. As her programme note states, the project

place the actor at the heart of generating material for performance. Stories, images and memories associated with a square foot chosen by each performer have found their forms through a series of interactions with creative artists working in different fields.[14]

Collaborating with artists from different disciplines, three performers had the opportunity to encounter different ways of working with their same chosen material, resulting in the devising of very different performances of that material.[15] As Hulton explains, each creative artist was to 'work with each "creative actor" to develop a small series of possible "forms" with each of them that will hold some of the "content" (ideas/associations/interests) that the "actor" was interested in exploring'.[16]

A second aim of *One Square Foot* was to explore the possibility of site for generating personal material, with the related question of how the performer might then retain this sense of site even when the performance was moved to a different site. The practical outcomes of the project were thus staged in two parts: in one, the ongoing performance-process work was shown 'on-site' to other participants in the project; in the other, the generated material was revised for a studio space and a public audience. This second focus of *One Square Foot* intersected with ongoing and still unresolved debates about the status of 'site' in so-called site-specific practice, itself not an entirely resolved term.[17]

If held against the 'purist' line early formulated by Richard Serra, who insisted that to move or relocate his work *Tilted Arc* (1981), would be 'to destroy the work',[18] *One Square Foot* might be considered less than site-specific. Yet as the various text-scripts of *One Square Foot: tree* clearly demonstrate, the work that came out of the chosen square foot was entirely dependent on that specific square foot. The facts, events, connections, histories, and people are all located in that square foot and their constellation could not have come about without that particular square foot. Or to be more precise, they could not have come about without my foot being in that square foot, because in some senses both the square foot and I, together, were the locus, nexus or conduit that made the various connections possible. In this performance, then, both the chosen square foot and 'I' are sites, and inarguably 'specific sites' without which this particular work could not have been made.[19] To have chosen a different square foot would have been to generate a different performance. Each step one takes literally moves one into a different set of potential narratives.

What parts of your body do you feel are related to your square foot?
Note them down. Write a short explanation of your choices.

Best Wishes, Arianna

The timescale of the project was tightly managed. Each of the three creative actors had chosen their square foot in advance of the artist-collaborators coming together in shared time and space, and each of the collaborators had sent preparatory tasks to the actors. However, the performers and artists would only have three sessions with each other where they could work together on generating further material and determining how to present this on-site to a small, invited audience. This stage of the project took a total of nine days.[20] The work generated and shown on-site was then 'moved' into a studio space, where it was revised and directed by Dorinda Hulton and Arianna Economou over a period of six days, in preparation for its public showing.

Mapping the Self

Site-body: Draw from your memory, feelings and knowledge of your square foot and create a spontaneous drawing A3 size in any media you like. [...]

Text-image: Look at your drawing and recollect a story related to your site. Write down 12 words during your process of reflection.

Yours, Horst

Journal Entry, June 2003: I collect leaves from the site, and make a stream-of-consciousness picture, writing a different word onto a leaf, 85 leaves in total (in homage to Sequoiah), all of them associated with my personal history and the history of the square foot. I randomly glue each of the leaves to an A3 canvas.[21]

Though Dorinda had her own set of research questions to be explored through practice, she had specifically invited me to be a performer-participant in the project because of my interest in autobiographical performance. *One Square Foot* gave me the opportunity to explore, through practice, some of the problematics I had encountered in thinking, writing and devising around autobiography, specifically the oft-repeated claim of autobiographical performance's narrow breadth of reference. Since moving to Exeter in 1998, and encountering the site-specific work of Wrights & Sites, I had also become increasingly interested in the relationship between site and autobiography, and had tentatively begun to explore this through deploying the term 'autotopography'.[22] Before turning to 'autotopography', it is useful to begin with the related and more familiar term 'autobiography'.

Object-memory: Choose a range of objects relevant to your site. Keep in mind the autobiographical significance as much as the material memory of your objects.

Horst

Journal Entry, June 2003: I plant a small fir tree in my old, well-worn, well-travelled shoe.

Auto: from the Greek, for Self, Same, One's own; *Bio*: from the Greek, *bios*, for life course, or way of living life; and *Graphy*, from the Greek, *graphein*, to scratch, to draw, to write. A commonsense understanding of autobiography is that it is the account, or recounting, of a life. The life, then, necessarily precedes the autobiography. However, post-structuralist theory prompts us to turn this conception on its head, understanding that there is no 'self' prior to its performance. The 'self' is a performative, reiterative act, inescapably bound up in the social and cultural discourses that permit certain selves to exist (while making other selves inconceivable and/or 'unreadable').

Autobiographical production is, of course, a creative act; an act of selecting, of ordering, of editing, of forgetting, of embellishing, of invention. Autobiography, then, rather than recounting a life already lived, in fact proposes or produces a certain life, a certain self. The production of autobiography is thus one means by which certain selves become reiterated and repeated. For example, as Sidonie Smith notes, autobiography traditionally provided a way of shoring up a belief in a 'deep' and 'inner' self, particularly the bourgeois subject.[23] This is the danger of all autobiographical production: the authorizing and authority that accrue to some selves, or some lives, at the expense of others. But it is also autobiography's political potential, because autobiography at least provides the space to write differently (albeit within and against the given parameters of any time and place). As more and more people access the autobiographical mode of production, picking up the autobiographical tools, more and more selves and possible lives are written and performed into existence. It is this ability or potential of autobiography to 'talk out' and to 'give voice' that has attracted me to it as a practice, a wilful and self-fashioning act. In writing and performing an autobiography, one becomes an agent, becomes active, becomes self-determining, choosing what stories to tell, what self to portray.

Sensations related to the present: 1. Put your ear to your square foot and write down a stream of consciousness. Include all the small 'stories', and fragments of 'stories' that you

can hear in your own head (like listening to a shell). Perhaps you could use sounds, parts of sentences, whispers, rumbles, grumbles, the sound of growth, of rotting, of small creatures moving, of stuff covered over...

Dorinda

Topos, from the Greek, for place; *Graphein*, to scratch, to draw, to write. Topography, then, is the writing of place. Adding *auto* to this mix is to admit the self that writes every place, since topography, like autobiography, is a creative act of interpretation, of perspective, of location. Places, like selves, are not simply given but are made. As geographer Tim Cresswell writes, 'places are constructed by people doing things and in this sense are never "finished" but are constantly being performed'.[24] I write place according to who I am as much as where I am; in fact, 'where' I am is as much to do with who I am as anything else. And arguably who I am is as much to do with where I am. Place and self are deeply imbricated, and both are contingent, shifting, always 'becoming'.

> Journal Entry, 24th August 2003: What is site if it is not always an interpretation, a perspective? (And in this collaborative project, that becomes plural.)

The 'writing' of place is as potentially reactionary or subversive as the 'writing' of self. Where an inclusive 'we' is often built on the foundations laid by the repetition of authorized (that is, acceptable and dominant) personal narratives, which serve to simultaneously construct a marginalized 'you', so the formation of 'place' can construct a fortress. One can easily feel 'out of place' by not knowing the 'proper' script.[25] However, as with all autobiographical production, place, as a performance, is nevertheless an event that 'provides the conditions of possibility for creative social practice'.[26] Greame Miller's *Linked* is a good example of the potential of 'autotopography' to rewrite, and in this instance, reclaim place. Miller's performance attempts to preserve place in memory and imagination. Though the physical locality might have been destroyed to make way for a motorway, the place continues to have an existence through the local stories. Such stories are necessary to (make) any place and also to (make) any self. Miller recognizes this deep link between place and self. As he astutely puts it,

> We write ourselves into the landscape. We own space because we can tell stories about it. And I thought that by making a narrative piece about the neighbourhood, I could put my life back on the map and re-appropriate ten years worth of memories that had been stolen.[27]

Miller not only put his life back on the map; he also put this specific place back on the map, in spite of its literal destruction.

Mike Pearson's *Bubbling Tom* might be considered yet another model of autotopographic performance practice. In the year 2000, it would seem that Lucy Lippard's 'lure of the local' made itself felt and reeled him in.[28] Participating in the national creative project *Small Acts: Performance, the Millennium and the Marking of Time*, Pearson chose to return to his 'home' of Hibaldstow, in Lincolnshire, and perform there for the first time.[29] Working with the evocative Welsh notion of 'y filltir sgwar', the square mile of our childhood, a place that we know intimately and 'in a detail we will never know anywhere again', Pearson's performance took place in ten sites that held childhood significance. The document of *Bubbling Tom*, though a different text to that of the live performance, nevertheless serves to suggest the multiplicity of 'tellings', 'selves' and places that Pearson performed. Just as his Nan's kitchen resounded with different types of talk, 'diverse discourses', all given equal footing, so too did *Bubbling Tom* juxtapose the factual with the fictional, event with imagination, history with story, narrative with fragment, past with present. In the guise of story-teller (and here Pearson is influenced by Walter Benjamin's story-teller),[30] Pearson wove 'together history, geography, genealogy, memoir and autobiography, and including anecdotes, traveller's tales, poetry, forensic data, quotations, lies, jokes, improvised asides, physical re-enactments, impersonations and intimate reflections'. Though each of Pearson's chosen locations could be marked on the OS Map of the area (such as SE 977760251), Pearson employed an 'older' form of mapmaking by literally plotting the landscape. Contrasting with more scientific cartography, which arguably conjures a fixed surface, a 'sphere of a completed horizontality',[31] Pearson's guided 'tour' transformed the fixed and anonymous coordinates into an inhabited and lively place. In 'returning home', what Pearson in fact brings home is that place, even supposedly local place, is multiple and therefore differently inhabited (putting the boundaries of 'local' into question).

Wishes related to the future:

1. Stand on your square foot and write a note for a stranger to read in the next ten seconds. How can you write it for them to read? Where can you write it?
2. Write a note for a stranger to read in the next hundred years. Is it possible to somehow leave that trace without disturbing your square foot? [...]

Dorinda

Meandering

Having only moved to Exeter in 1998, choosing a square foot that had some significance was, in fact, quite difficult. Had the project been located in Glasgow, I would have had more square feet to choose from. A square foot in the first place I lived when I left home, aged 17, to attend Glasgow University (the big city). A square foot in any of the houses I lived subsequently, each one testimony to a different moment in my life (friends, boyfriends, girlfriends, breakups, degrees, jobs). Somehow, the events associated with my younger selves seemed more significant. And the fact that I had lived for thirteen years in Glasgow, but for only five in Exeter, also seemed to make a difference (Lippard's 'lure of the local' again?). I did not, yet, feel any deep significance for any place in Exeter, other than my place of work or the pub located across the road from it, neither of which promised much in the way of devising a performance, partly because the *One Square Foot* project offered an escape from that everyday world.

Given that my partner of eight years still lived in Glasgow, one place that did hold some significance for me, literally and metaphorically, was Exeter St Davids – the train station where I would habitually board the Virgin train bound for Glasgow, typically arriving 'home' eight to ten hours later. As most site-practitioners can testify, one of the biggest challenges of making the work is securing the site, and this was to be no exception. Health and Safety regulations meant that any performance on the platform would be out of the question, as would any performance within a certain distance of the train track. Permission would, in the first instance, have to be sought from Railtrack. Given that any space I chose would have to be able to accommodate at least fifteen invited spectators, the options around 'Exeter St Davids' were becoming increasingly limited and less attractive.

For two years prior to making *One Square Foot* I had been a warden in a Halls of Residence. I was fortunate enough to have been allocated a small hall, with a total of 35 students housed in an old Georgian manor. Though the house was in some disrepair (and has, in fact, been subsequently 'decommissioned'), the landscaped gardens in which it was located were immaculately maintained. At the rear of these gardens was a huge tree, under which was a bench. Though not located far from the house, for some reason the students never seemed to wander into this section of the garden. For this reason, it became my place of respite during my wardenship, the place I would come when I wanted a bit of peace. This place also became my chosen square foot.

4. *Imagine the worst thing that could happen to your square foot. Write about it. [...]*

Dorinda

Just before the project begins, I confront a devastating sight. The 'bench', upon which I sit, under the tree, is lying in pieces on the ground. Smashed. I pick up one of the pieces and carry it home with me. This is a fragment of my sanctuary. I am not sure if I am keeping it, or myself, safe. This is not, though, I realise, the worst thing. That would be to turn the corner and see the stub of a trunk, surrounded by sawdust, like spilt blood. (My father was a forester.)

Though the initial choice of my square foot had been made purely on its significance in my present, everyday life, creative provocations sent by each artist enabled me to reconceive this small square of land as being depthful and layered; as existing simultaneously in the present and the past (and also conjuring a future); as being literally here, but also someplace else – in fact, many other places; as being personal (micro) but also connected to others (macro); as continuously shifting.

> Journal Entry, 15th July 2003: Horst and I gather cones from underneath the Sequoia. We cover my square foot in them, making a square foot of cones. We also make a trail of leaves, running from the trunk of the tree, trailing off into the grove. On each leaf, I write a word, duplicating the words from the 85 I had earlier written for my own talking leaves, my autobiographical lexicon. We will leave these, and the cones, overnight. We have no control over our material tonight, cannot plan what tomorrow will bring, because it may depend on the events of tonight.

The place of my square foot is, despite appearances, mobile; it is continuously and simultaneously moving across time and space. This is not the place of some 'origin' or 'authenticity', whether of experience or belonging. My square foot, though bounded in its actual size (144 square inches) is infinite in its potential reach and breadth. It is difficult to know where the 'limit' or the 'outside' might lie, or even if there is one.

Yet the square foot also, at the same time, remains an anchor, the coordinate around which the other stories coalesce. Both/and becomes my way of working with what appears to be a contradiction. I have a foot in the 'local', but that same foot is also in the 'global'. My story is also the story of others and other places. Both rooted and moving; both roots and routes. This is not so dissimilar to my understanding of identity and self; both fictional and lived; discursive yet nevertheless 'real' (really affected by sexism, heterosexism, etc.). For geographer Doreen Massey, 'what gives a place its specificity is not some long internalized history but the fact that it is constructed out of a particular constellation of social relations, meeting and weaving together at a particular locus'.[32] Standing in the square foot, the 'particular locus' is both the land and my self, but at the same time, this place and my self are themselves 'constructed out of a particular constellation of social relations'.

Journal Entry, Wednesday 16th July 2003: So the first thing to record is the effect of nature/passing of time on our installation. I was quite, quite amazed at the transformation that had taken place overnight. Whilst the cones were more or less in the same configurations, the actual cones had changed considerably. When we had laid the cones out yesterday, they had been open and a sort of reddy brown colour. They were round in shape, full. This morning, they were all silvery white and had closed up. Helen remarked that it looked as if the cones, having been moved, were now reacting to this new and unknown environment by protecting themselves, closing up and becoming smaller. The trail of leaves [that I had laid] had also been interrupted so that it was now fragmented. Some of the leaves had been blown away or blown over. Others had been blown out of the sequence.

The specific 'weave' of interconnected routes, like the actual woven roots of the Sequoia tree (the 'family tree' seen from a different perspective?), goes something like this: tree–father–Sequoia–Sequoiah–Cherokee–trail of tears–Glasgow–Exeter–California–India–Strathnaven–alphabet–Gaelic–childhood ...[33] Again quoting Massey,

> what if space is the sphere not of a discrete, multiplicity of inert things, even one which is thoroughly interrelated? What if, instead, it presents us with a heterogeneity of practices and processes? Then it will be not an already-interconnected whole but an ongoing product of interconnections and not. Then it will always be unfinished and open. This arena of space is not firm ground on which to stand. In no way is it a surface.[34]

My square foot, then, is not a surface but rather 'an arena of space'. Reading this, I also hazard to guess that we could productively replace 'space' with self, and arrive at the same exhilarating proposition. In One Square Foot I am simultaneously writing self as much as place, writing each through the other.

4. *Listening. As you listen to the sounds surrounding your square foot, become aware of which parts of your body are affected/touched by the sounds. Feel how the sounds reach your body and through which areas. Which part of your body is touched by, or massaged by which sound?*
5. *Translate the sounds that surround you into movement.*

Arianna

Journal Entry, 7th June 2003: I hear the sound of birds. I hear the sound of someone cutting a tree, in the distance, the flesh offering little resistance. I hear the sound of a train. It might be the train to Glasgow, my train 'home'.

Standing Still
Does it strike you as odd that this exploration of a single, square foot appears in a collection that is ostensibly about 'walking'?

Touch your square foot and describe what you feel. Touch it at different times of the day and in different weathers. Dig into it if you can. Stand on it. Describe what you can feel against your skin and with different parts of your body.

Dorinda

In his contribution to this collection, Lavery has provided a thorough account of 'walking practices', from the art of walking epitomized in Fulton's and Long's work, to the challenge of walking issued by the flâneur and the later situationists, which feed into the more recent incarnation of walking practices as found in the work of Wrights & Sites and Lone Twin.[35] We have also encountered various 'theories' of walking, from Debord to de Certeau to Solnit. The phenomenologists celebrate the experiential quality of walking, with Solnit summarizing Edmund Husserl's work when she writes that 'it is the body that moves but the world that changes', an experience which enables us to retain a sense of a coherent self amidst 'the flux of the world'.[36] Walking, the literal contact of body with environment, supposedly provides a privileged mode of knowledge. But what about the potential art or aesthetic of standing still, a philosophy or phenomenology of being stationary? What if, rather than walking through place, one stops in place? If walking is seen as an implicit protest against the speed by which we (are forced to) live our contemporary lives, an activity in opposition to 'fast transport', then choosing to resist movement altogether might be even more radical.

In this context, being stationary is to be differentiated from the frustrated 'waiting' acknowledged by Lavery. Standing still, here, is an active choice rather than an enforced in-between point on a journey from A to B. Standing still is to have arrived.

Stand on your square foot and find the most interesting direction in which to look. What is in your direct line of vision? What is on the periphery?

Dorinda

Standing still allows the time to look and listen and feel a-round, literally taking a 360 degree perspective; to look above and below; to look inside and out; to look and look again. Isn't this also what the flâneurs were up to? Standing still and really looking; standing still as an action. This is purposeful lingering, good lingering (and not, then, malingering).[37] Perhaps, though, the perceived danger of standing still is that you become rooted to the spot. However, while I am in one square foot (rather than roaming one square mile), in fact I find myself travelling across centuries and continents, in the company of new acquaintances, acquaintances met precisely because by standing still time was made for our paths to cross. Standing still, I travel from Exeter to Glasgow to India to California to Georgia and Oklahoma, to Strathnaven, and 'home' again; from 2003 to 1998 to 1821 to 1838 to 1814.

Each imaginary step through time and place is taken by another 'me'. 'I' am in flux. Standing still, against all predictions or assumptions, in fact has enabled an 'extroverted' performance.[38]

If , as David Williams proposes, 'to walk the story is to attend to landscape as inscape, and to take (a) place in the world',[39] perhaps to not walk but to stand in one spot is paradoxically to attend to landscape as ex-scape (or as escape from the self). Standing still, prompted by the multiple sights of this one site, my self wanders (off), leaving others in my wake. Rooted and moving; roots and routes.

> Journal Entry, Saturday 19th July 2003: Arianne now feels that standing and walking are all that is needed.

> Journal Entry, Sunday 20th July 2003: The walking and standing should continue throughout the whole piece.

Movement, culturally, is often equated with liberation and adventure (an outward lookingness) whereas to stay put is deemed conservative and safe (a narrow-mindedness). Such celebrations of movement need to take notice of context, particularly when movement has been an enforced situation for many, throughout history. Equally, not all are 'free' to move, with borders and checks making staying put the only available option. Reading 'movement' as implicitly liberatory and 'staying put' as intrinsically reactionary neglects the difference made by specific details that lead to 'variegated texture[s] of habitation'.[40]

One Square Foot: tree does in fact include a significant walk within its text – the murderous walk undertaken by the Cherokee Indians as they were forcibly removed from their land. This 'trail of

tears' offers a counter-balance to idealistic notions of walking as being radical or oppositional and reminds us that walking (and standing still) is always a context-bound activity. Ahmed *et al.* also remind us that within a context of globalization, *'being grounded is not necessarily about being fixed; being mobile is not necessarily about being detached'*.[41]

> *Stand outside your square foot and watch what happens to it when you're not on it?*
> *Describe what you see...the changing light on it, people moving over it...*
>
> *Dorinda*

Walking

It is not, in any case, quite accurate to say that there was no literal walking in *One Square Foot: tree*. In addition to the enforced walking of the Cherokees in 1838, all of the various versions of *One Square Foot: tree* involved some element of walking. Working with installation artist Horst Weierstall, we set a paper trail for our spectators, leading from a road by the Halls of Residence to the tree. Each piece of paper was imprinted on both sides with different words chosen from the lexicon of 85 words that I had devised. At the tree itself, I walked repeatedly along a length of string tied to the trunk, moving paper words along it, the tree my starting and finishing point. I also walked the circumference of what seemed like a natural circle in front of the tree, a space resembling an amphitheatre (or the edge of the globe?) The performance from beginning to end was structured around walking. In my work with choreographer Arianna Economou, the whole performance was improvised around the dual activities of walking and standing still, listening to the inner and outer prompts, shuttling between self and other, here and there. And finally, with director and dramaturge Dorinda Hulton, the space itself, and our movement through it, became a dramaturgical device for the sequencing of text. Prior to working with me on site, Hulton had made her own site-visit, mapping out its possibilities with the threads of overheard stories in her mind's eye.

> Journal Entry, Wednesday 24th July 2003: Behind the Sequoia, Dorinda discovered the open flat playing field. Then she saw the grove, and it reminded her of a Native American landscape in a way. And then she walked back to the Sequoia, and had always been interested in the little tree growing opposite it, so thought this might be another place on the journey, whatever the journey was.

Working with Hulton, we walked away from the square foot and, as Hulton commented, 'the landscape travelled through in the physical journey matched, like a faint, sensate echo, the landscapes within the journeys narrated'.[42] Through our initial exploratory walking (and stopping), the 'journey' or pattern of the text began to take shape, as we discovered what worked where. By working with text in place, we were enabled to make dramaturgical choices, with the literal route determining the textual route. The site became, in a way, the judicial editor, making the decisions for us. The site also carried its own linguistic equivalent. In Hulton's own words,

> Guided by the physical situation of the square foot, a dramaturgical structure, or map, emerged suggesting also its own kind of grammar and punctuation, changes in direction for example, marking the juxtaposition of one text with another as a new paragraph might; a walk between two resting points becoming the dramatic equivalent of a suspensory pause inviting time to reflect on the last image and to wonder about the next; leaving the spinney feeling like a semi colon, crossing the ditch like a comma, standing around the little tree at the end of the piece like a dot dot dot...[43]

The 'pattern' of the physical journey, and the resulting dramaturgical structure of the text, also provided us with a way to move the piece off-site.

Just as the route walked on-site had taken the shape of a circle, albeit starting at two opposite points (the large Sequoia tree and the small sapling standing opposite it), in the studio I walked my routes and narratives out in a repeating circle, each circle mirroring my own migration, those of the Cherokees, and of the Scottish people moved from their land during the clearances. My walk in the studio ended, like the performance on-site, not in my square foot, but facing it, looking across at the Sequoia that had been my place of respite and the initial source of my subsequent travel, looking across time and space not as a layered sedimentation (here and there, past and present), but rather as a coeval network of forged connections.[44] Of course, in the studio space, my square foot was not literally there. However, having spent so much time standing on it, I felt that I carried it, and the stories I had mapped, with me into this new space. Rooted and moving.

Views

Journal Entry, 28th August 2003: What drove my selection of stories was precisely to do with how much this site could be opened up, in order to let others in, in order to communicate beyond itself (and it is really 'myself'), in order to go from this very local, very specific, to a more global history (and this is a history of consequence, of implication, of reckoning).

In thinking about the work that autobiographical performance does, performer Tim Miller has proposed that it should construct a window for the spectator, allowing them a way into the performer's life and experiences.[45] I like to think that the square foot is just such a window; not only onto my life and experiences, but onto a whole host of other bodies and places. The *One Square Foot* project offers one model for making an autobiographical performance that inevitably goes beyond the self, because the site itself becomes a co-author and co-subject. Without the site, the narratives would not have been identified in the first place. Moreover, the square foot leads you on totally unexpected journeys, for you cannot predict where you will end up, nor what you will find under the soles of your feet.

Professor J. Anderson (Consultant Ecologist):

This is one of the paradoxes of soil. People look at a soil and just see that structure and nothing more, but it is in fact an incredible microcosm of life. There's more diversity of organism living below ground than there are above ground [...]. If we were to think of the microbes, if we were to do an analysis of the bacteria in a [small] area like that [pointing to a small section of the square foot], there's probably several thousand species of bacteria, some of which will be new to science, just within that tiny amount of organic matter.

As video artist and documenter Peter Hulton so perceptively put it, one square foot is infinite in its potential. I suspect that one millimetre might be equally so, with only the tip of your finger used to mark the spot of connection. In Massey's words,

This is space as the sphere of a dynamic simultaneity, constantly disconnected by new arrivals, constantly waiting to be determined (and therefore always undertermined) by the construction of new relations. It is always being made and always therefore, in a sense, unfinished (except that 'finishing' is not on the agenda). If you were to take a slice through time it would be full of holes, of disconnections, of tentative half-formed first encounters. [...] Loose ends and ongoing stories.[46]

Roots and routes. Rooted and moving.

Journal Entry, 28th August 2003: It will take you in ways that you could never dream of, open up stories and lives that are so far beyond yourself, yet still tap into yourself [....]

Notes

1. An earlier version of this writing has been published in *PAJ: A Journal of Performance and Art*, Spring 2007. Since writing this reflection I have also published the monograph, *Autobiography and Performance* (Basingstoke: Palgrave Macmillan, 2008).

2. Sidonie Smith and Julia Watson (eds), *Getting a Life: Everyday Uses of Autobiography* (Minneapolis: University of Minnesota Press, 1996), p. 9.

3. Cathy Turner, 'Framing the Site', *Site-Specific: The Quay Thing Documented, Studies in Theatre and Performance*, Supplement 5, 2000, p. 24.

4. ibid. I kept a journal throughout the project, recording not only the actions undertaken, but also my feelings about them. This journal documented my role as a creative actor. Had I known I would be writing this chapter, here and now, I would have kept a different sort of journal. Documentation of the project, including commentary by the project's director, Dorinda Hulton, the journals kept by each creative actor, and recordings of the different performances (on-site and in the studio), exist in DVD-Rom format. See *One Square Foot: An Exploration into Interdisciplinary Performer Training*, DVD-Rom, Arts Documentation Unit, 2004.

5. Mike Pearson and Michael Shanks, *Theatre/Archaeology: Disciplinary Dialogues* (London: Routledge, 2001).

6. Inserted text, italicized in format, is taken from instructions sent by each creative artist.

7. See my article, 'The Politics of the Personal: Autobiography in Performance', in Elaine Aston and Geraldine Harris (eds), *Feminist Futures?* (London: Palgrave Macmillan, 2007), pp. 130–48.

8. Geraldine Harris, *Staging Femininities: Performance and Performativity* (Manchester: Manchester University Press, 1999), p. 167.

9. Lisa Kron, interview with the author, September 2004. Lisa Kron is a member of the New York performance group The Five Lesbian Brothers and has also made a number of autobiographical works, including *101 Humiliating Stories*, *2.5 Minute Ride* and *Well*.

10. Bonnie Marranca, 'The Self as Text: Uses of Autobiography in the Theatre (Animations as Model)', *Performing Arts Journal*, 1979/80, 10/11, 4(1/2), pp. 85–105.

11. Ruth Weisberg, *Artweek*, 22 November 1980; cited in Moira Roth (ed.), *Rachel Rosenthal* (Baltimore: The John Hopkins University Press, 1997), p. 107.

12. Professor J. Anderson works at the University of Exeter. His brief visual analyses of each of the square feet is recorded on *One Square Foot*, DVD-Rom.

13. See Dorinda Hulton, 'The Creative Actor', in Christopher McCullough (ed.), *Theatre Praxis* (London: Macmillan, 1998); Dorinda Hulton, 'Joseph Chaikin', in Alison Hodge (ed.), *Actor Training in the Twentieth Century* (London: Routledge, 1999).

14. Dorinda Hulton, Programme, *One Square Foot*, 2003.

15. The other performers were Daniel Jamieson and Jordan Whyte.

16. Dorinda Hulton, *One Square Foot*, DVD-Rom.

17. Fiona Wilkie, 'Mapping the Terrain: a Survey of Site-Specific Performance in Britain', *New Theatre Quarterly*, 70, 2002, pp. 140–60.

18. Cited in Miwon Kwon, *One Place After Another: Site-Specific Art and Locational Identity* (Cambridge, Massachusetts: MIT Press, 2004), p. 12.

19. In the same way, Daniel Jamieson's and Jordan Whyte's performances arose from the combination of their specifically created 'selves' in their specifically chosen square feet. Their performances were titled *One Square Foot: footway* and *One Square Foot: a map of the gardens*.

20. At the showings on site, company members from Theatre Alibi were invited. Other spectators included all the artist-collaborators and the creative actors.

21. All such citations are taken from my reflective journal, written during the project.

22. First working with this term in 2000, I subsequently became aware of its different, yet related application by Jennifer González who uses it to refer to personal objects – such as photos, tourist memorabilia, etc. – arranged by a subject as physical signs that spatially represent that subject's identity. See Jennifer González, 'Autotopographies', in Gabriel Brahm Jr and Martin Driscoll (eds), *Prosthetic Territories. Politics and Hypertechnologies* (San Francisco: Westview Press, 1995), pp. 133–50. In my application of the term autotopography, the *topos* is taken more literally (problematic as any concept of 'real' place is).

23. Sidonie Smith and Julia Watson (eds), *Women, Autobiography, Theory: A Reader* (Madison: University of Wisconsin Press, 1998), p. 110.

24. Tim Cresswell, *Place: A Short Introduction* (London: Blackwell, 2004), p. 37.

25. See Tim Cresswell's 'moral geographies' in *In Place/Out of Place: Geography, Ideology and Transgression* (Minneapolis: University of Minnesota Press, 1996).

26. Cresswell, *Place*, p. 39.

27. Cited in Carl Lavery, 'Walking the Walk, Talking the Talk: Re-imagining the Urban Landscape; Graeme Miller interviewed by Carl Lavery', *New Theatre Quarterly*, 21(2), May 2005, p. 161.

28. Lucy Lippard, *The Lure of the Local: Senses of Place in a Multicentered Society* (New York: The New Press, 1997).

29. Mike Pearson, 'Bubbling Tom', in Adrian Heathfield (ed.), *Small Acts: Performance, the Millennium and the Marking of Time* (London: Black Dog Publishing, 2000), pp. 175–81. See also Deirdre Heddon, 'Performing the Archive: Following in the Footsteps', *Performance Research: On Archives*, 7(4), 2002, pp. 172–85.

30. Walter Benjamin, *Illuminations*, Hannah Arendt (ed.) (New York: Schocken Books, 1968).

31. Doreen Massey, *For Space* (London: Sage Publications, 2005), p. 107.

32. Doreen Massey, 'A Global Sense of Place', in Trevor Barnes and Derek Gregory (eds), *Reading Human Geography: The Poetics and Politics* (London: Arnold, 1997), pp. 315–23; originally published in *Marxism Today*, June 1991, pp. 24–29.

33. I am aware of Felix Guattari's and Gilles Deleuze's concept of the 'rhizome', an oppositional term and model to that of 'tree' and 'roots', and there is undoubtedly a parallel between the process of *One Square Foot: tree*, and the connections made within it, to the non-hierarchal rhizomic structure proposed by Guattari and Deleuze. The idea of being both rooted and moving, and of roots and routes, as explored in this performance, is undoubtedly motivated by my own desire to locate different ways of being in constellation with others. However, it would have seemed paradoxical to site my performance under a tree, on its roots, and then work in opposition to trees/roots. I wonder whether there might be more productive ways to consider the structure of 'trees' that do not limit it to notions of hierarchy? In fact, as Professor Anderson's comments on the ecology of trees suggests,

the actual tree (rather than the tree as a symbol for the organization of information) is in a symbiotic relationship with millions of other organisms. See Guattari and Deleuze, *A Thousand Plateaus: Capitalism and Schizophrenia* (Minneapolis: University of Minnesota Press, 1987).

34. Massey, *For Space*, p. 107.

35. It is worth noting that the 'walking' practitioners most often cited are men. Though attempts have been made to generate the figure of the *flâneuse*, other critics have stressed the point that the specularity of *flânery* implicitly disbarred women since they were always the object of the (male) gaze, and never its subject (see Priscilla Parkhurst Ferguson, 'The *flâneur* On and Off the Streets of Paris', in Keith Tester (ed.), *The Flâneur* (London: Routledge, 1994), pp. 22–42; Doreen Massey, 'Flexible Sexism', *Environment and Planning D: Society and Space*, 1991, 9, pp. 31–57). Place is always political, and each body inhabits it differently. As Elspeth Probyn pointedly reminds us, 'space is a pressing matter and it matters which bodies, where and how, press up against it' ('Lesbians in Space. Gender, Sex and the Structure of Missing', *Gender, Place and Culture*, 2(1), 1995, pp. 77–84). If I were Carl, my mourning walk might be more distracted, and less of a ritual, as I am compelled to keep looking over my shoulders just to make sure I am not being followed. This might just be me, of course, but I suspect not. My current research project (2008/9), undertaken in collaboration with Wrights & Sites member, Cathy Turner, is focused on exploring the walking practices of contemporary women artists.

36. Rebecca Solnit, *Wanderlust: A History of Walking* (New York: Viking, 2000), p. 27. Note that the 2001 British edition is listed in this book's bibliography.

37. Thanks to Phil Smith for an engaging discussion on lingering/malingering at PSI 12, Queen Mary University, London, 12 July 2006.

38. Massey, *For Space*.

39. David Williams, 'Frontwords', *Performance Research: On Place*, 3(2), 1998, p. vii.

40. Sara Ahmed, Claudia Castañeda, Anne-Marie Fortier, Mimi Sheller (eds), *Uprootings/Regroundings: Questions of Home and Migration* (Oxford & New York: Berg, 2003).

41. ibid., p. 1; original emphasis.

42. Dorinda Hulton, 'Site as source and resource', unpublished paper presented at the symposium 'Site/ Sight <=> Source/Resource', Exeter University, 2004.

43. ibid.

44. See Massey, *For Space*.

45. Tim Miller, interview with the author, November 2002. Tim Miller is a gay performance artist who has made many solo, autobiographical shows, including *My Queer Body* and *Glory Box*.

46. Massey, *For Space*, p. 107.

SOURCES

Adorno, Theodor W. and Max Horkheimer. *Dialectic of Enlightenment* (London: Verso, 1997).

Ahmed, Sara, Claudia Castañeda, Anne-Marie Fortier and Mimi Sheller (eds). *Uprootings/Regroundings: Questions of Home and Migration* (Oxford & New York: Berg, 2003).

Anderson, Linda. *Autobiography* (London & New York: Routledge, 2001).

Augé, Marc. *Non-Places: A Geography of Supermodernity* (London: Verso, 1995).

Austin, Clive and Phil Smith. *Drift (155)*, DVD UK PAL (Totnes: thejauntycontinuum, 2005); also *Videomission* [online] http://www.videomission.net/?video=d8bfa146093d3eab52b507b573324bc9; *Rhizomes* 13, Fall 2006 [online] http://www.rhizomes.net/issue13/smith/index.html.

Bachelard, Gaston. *The Poetics of Reverie: Childhood, Language and the Cosmos* (Boston: Beacon Press, 1991).

Bachelard, Gaston. *The Poetics of Space* (Boston: Beacon Press, 1969).

Bal, Mieke. 'Introduction', in Mieke Bal, Jonathan Crewe and Leo Spitzer (eds). *Acts of Memory: Cultural Recall in the Present* (Hanover: University Press of New England, 1999).

Benjamin, Walter. *Illuminations*, Hannah Arendt (ed.) (New York: Schocken Books, 1968).

Bhabha, Homi. 'The Third Space', interview in Jonathan Rutherford (ed.), *Identity: Community, Culture, Difference* (London: Lawrence & Wishart, 1990).

Bhabha, Homi. *Location of Culture* (London: Routledge, 1994).

Blackmore, Susan. *The Meme Machine* (Oxford: Oxford University Press, 1999).

Borden, Iain, Jane Rendell, Joe Kerr with Alicia Pivaro (eds). *The Unknown City: Contesting Architecture and Social Space* (Cambridge, Mass.: The MIT Press, 2001).

Boym, Svetlana. *The Future of Nostalgia* (New York: Basic Books, 2001).

Bradby, Lawrence and Carl Lavery. 'Moving Through Place: Itinerant Performance and the Search for a Community of Reverie', *Research in Drama Education*, 12(1), February 2007, pp. 41–54.

Bürger, Peter. *Theory of the Avant-Garde* (Manchester: Manchester University Press, 1984).

Careri, Francesco. *Walkscapes: Walking as an Aesthetic Practice* (Barcelona: Gustavo Gili, 2002).

Carlson, Allen. *Aesthetics and the Environment: The Appreciation of Art, Nature and Architecture* (London: Routledge, 2000).

Cavendish, Margaret. *The Blazing World and Other Writings* (London: Penguin, 1994).

de Certeau, Michel. *The Practice of Everyday Life* (Berkeley: University of California Press, 1984).

de Certeau, Michel. 'Walking in the City', in Gary Bridge and Sophie Watson (eds), *The Blackwell City Reader* (Oxford: Blackwell, 2002), pp. 381–92.

Chaudhuri, Una and Elinor Fuchs (eds). *Land/Scape/Theater* (Ann Arbor: University of Michigan Press, 2002).

Conquergood, Dwight. 'Performance Studies: Interventions and Radical Research', in Henry Bial (ed.), *The Performance Studies Reader* (London & New York: Routledge, 2004).

Cosgrove, Denis. *Social Formation and Symbolic Landscape* (London: Croon Helm, 1984).

Cresswell, Tim. *In Place/Out of Place: Geography, Ideology and Transgression* (Minneapolis: University of Minnesota Press, 1996).

Cresswell, Tim. *Place: A Short Introduction* (London: Blackwell, 2004).

Darby, Wendy Joy. *Landscape and Identity: Geographies of Nation and Class in England* (Oxford & New York: Berg, 2000).

Debord, Guy. *The Society of the Spectacle* (Detroit: Black and Red, 1983).

Dolan, Jill. *Utopia in Performance: Finding Hope at the Theater* (Ann Arbor: University of Michigan Press, 2005).

Evans, Mary. *Missing Persons: The Impossibility of Auto/biography* (London & New York: Routledge, 1999).

Freeman, Anthony. *Consciousness: A Guide to the Debates* (Santa Barbara: ABC-CLIO, Inc., 2003).

Fulton, Hamish. 'Into a Walk into Nature', in Jeffrey Kastner and Brian Wallis (eds), *Land and Environmental Art* (London: Phaidon, 1998).

Fulton, Hamish. *Walking Artist* (Düsseldorf: Richter, 2001).

Ferguson, Priscilla Parkhurst. 'The *flâneur* On and Off the Streets of Paris', in Keith Tester (ed.), *The Flâneur* (London: Routledge, 1994), 22–42.

Garner, Stanton B. 'Urban Landscapes, Theatrical Encounters: Staging the City', in Una Chaudhuri and Elinor Fuchs (eds), *Land/Scape/Theater* (Ann Arbor: University of Michigan Press, 2002), pp. 94–118.

Gibson, James J. *The Senses Considered as Perceptual Systems* (London: George Allen & Unwin, 1968).

Gibson, James J. *The Perception of The Visual World* (Cambridge, Mass.: The Riverside Press, 1950).

Gilbert-Rolfe, Jeremy. *Beauty and the Contemporary Sublime* (New York: Allworth Press, 1999).

González, Jennifer. 'Autotopographies', in Gabriel Brahm Jr and Martin Driscoll (eds), *Prosthetic Territories. Politics and Hypertechnologies* (San Francisco: Westview Press, 1995), pp. 133–50.

Graham, Stephen. *The Gentle Art of Tramping* (London: Ernest Benn, 1929).

Guattari, Felix and Gilles Deleuze. *A Thousand Plateaus: Capitalism and Schizophrenia* (Minneapolis: University of Minnesota Press, 1987).

Harris, Geraldine. *Staging Femininities: Performance and Performativity* (Manchester: Manchester University Press, 1999).

Heddon, Deirdre. *Autobiography and Performance* (Basingstoke: Palgrave Macmillan, 2008).

Heddon, Deirdre E. 'Autotopography: Graffiti, Landscapes & Selves', *Reconstruction*, 2(3), Summer 2002, [online] http://reconstruction.eserver.org/023/heddon.htm.

Heddon, Deirdre. 'One Square Foot: Thousands of Roots', *PAJ: A Journal of Performance and Art*, 86, 29(2), May 2007, pp. 40–50.

Heddon, Deirdre. 'Performing Lesbians: Constructing the Self, Constructing the Community', in Maggie B. Gale and Viv Gardner (eds), *Auto/biography and Identity: Women, Theatre and Performance* (Manchester & New York: Manchester University Press, 2004).

Heddon, Deirdre. 'Performing the Archive: Following in the Footsteps', *Performance Research: On Archives*, 7(4), 2002, pp. 172–85.

Heddon, Deirdre. 'The Politics of the Personal: Autobiography in Performance', in Elaine Aston and Geraldine Harris (eds), *Feminist Futures?* (London: Palgrave Macmillan, 2007), pp. 130–48.

Hetherington, Kevin. *The Badlands of Modernity: Heterotopia and Social Ordering* (London & New York: Routledge, 1997).

Highmore, Ben. *Cityscapes* (London and New York: Routledge, 2005).

Hill, Leslie and Helen Paris (eds). *Performance and Place* (Basingstoke: Palgrave Macmillan, 2006).

Hodge, Alison (ed.) *Actor Training in the Twentieth Century* (London: Routledge, 1999).

Hulton, Dorinda. 'The Creative Actor', in Christopher McCullough (ed.), *Theatre Praxis: Teaching Drama Through Practice* (London: Palgrave Macmillan, 1998).

Hulton, Dorinda. *One Square Foot: An Exploration into Interdisciplinary Performer Training*, DVD-Rom (Exeter: Arts Documentation Unit, 2004).

Huyssen, Andreas. 'Trauma and Memory: A New Imaginary of Temporality', in Jill Bennett and Roseanne Kennedy (eds), *World Memory: Personal Trajectories in Global Time* (London: Palgrave Macmillan, 2003).

Ingold, Tim. 'Globes and Spheres: The Topology of Environmentalism', in Kay Milton (ed.), *Environmentalism: The View from Anthropology* (London & New York, Routledge, 1993).

Ingold, Tim. *The Perception of the Environment: Essays in Livelihood, Dwelling and Skill* (London: Routledge, 2000).

Jakovljevic, Branislav. 'The Space Specific Theatre: Skewed Visions' *The City Itself* ', *The Drama Review*, 49(3), 2005, pp. 96–106.

Janz, Bruce B. (ed.) *Research on Place and Space* [online] http://pegasus.cc.ucf.edu/~janzb/place/.

Kastner, Jeffrey (ed.) *Land and Environmental Art* (London: Phaidon Press, 1998).

Kaye, Nick. *Site-Specific Art: Performance, Place and Documentation* (London: Routledge, 2000).

Keiller, Patrick. 'Popular Science', in Ann Gallagher (ed.), *Landscape* (London: British Council, 2001), pp. 60–67.

Keiller, Patrick. 'A Conversation Between Patrick Wright and Patrick Keiller', in *London* and *Robinson in Space*, pamphlet accompanying *Robinson in Space* (2005), dir. P. Keiller, 78 mins (London: BFI), pp. 1–30.

Kelso, J.A. Scott. *Dynamic Patterns: The Self-Organization of Brain and Behaviour* (Cambridge, Mass.: MIT Press, 1997).

Kemal, Salim and Ivan Gaskell (eds). *Landscape, Natural Beauty and the Arts* (Cambridge: Cambridge University Press, 1995).

King, James. *Interior Landscapes: A Life of Paul Nash* (London: Weidenfeld & Nicolson, 1987).

Knabb, Ken (ed.) *Situationist International Anthology* (Berkeley CA: Bureau of Public Secrets, 1981).

Kobialka, Michal. 'Deleria/Nostalgia; Time, Space, Topography', in Judie Christie, Richard Gough and Daniel Watt (eds), *A Performance Cosmology: Testimony from the Future, Evidence of the Past* (Abingdon: Routledge, 2006).

Kwon, Miwon. *One Place After Another: Site-Specific Art and Locational Identity* (Cambridge, Mass.: MIT Press, 2004).

Lavery, Carl. 'The Pepys of E11: The Politics of *Linked*', *New Theatre Quarterly*, 21:2, 2005, pp. 148–60.

Lavery, Carl. 'Walking the Walk: Talking the Talk, Re-imagining the Urban Landscape – An Interview with Graeme Miller', *New Theatre Quarterly*, 21:2, 2005, pp. 161–65.

Lefebvre, Henri. *Writings on Cities*, Eleonore Kofman and Elizabeth Lebas (trans. and eds) (Oxford: Blackwell, 2003).

Levy, David J. *Hans Jonas: The Integrity of Thinking* (Columbia: University of Missouri Press, 2002).

Lippard, Lucy R. *The Lure of the Local: Senses of Place in a Multi-centered Society* (New York: New Press, 1997).

Machen, Arthur. *Things Near and Far* (London: Martin Secker, 1923).

Machen, Arthur. *The London Adventure or The Art of Wandering* (London: Martin Secker, 1924).

Mackey, Sally and Nicolas Whybrow. Editorial and Introduction, 'Taking Place: Some Reflections on Site, Performance and Community', *Research in Drama Education*, 12(1), February 2007, pp. 1–14.

Macnulty, W. Kirk. *The Way of the Craftsman* (Hinckley: Central Regalia, 2002).

Marcus, Laura. *Auto/biographical Discourses: Theory, Criticism, Practice* (Manchester: Manchester University Press, 1994).

Marranca, Bonnie. *Ecologies of Theatre: Essays at the Century Turning* (Baltimore: John Hopkins, 1995).

Marranca, Bonnie. 'The Self as Text: Uses of Autobiography in the Theatre (Animations as Model)', *Performing Arts Journal*, 1979/80, 10/11, 4(1/2), pp. 85–105.

Massey, Doreen. 'Flexible Sexism', *Environment and Planning D: Society and Space*, 1991, 9, pp. 31–57.

Massey, Doreen. *For Space* (London: Sage Publications, 2005).

Massey, Doreen. 'A Global Sense of Place', in Trevor Barnes and Derek Gregory (eds), *Reading Human Geography: The Poetics and Politics* (London: Arnold, 1997), pp. 315–23.

Massey, Doreen. 'Power-geometry and a Progressive Sense of Place', in Jon Bird, Barry Curtis, Tim Putnam, George Robertson and Lisa Tickner (eds), *Mapping the Futures* (London & New York: Routledge, 1993).

Massey, Doreen. *Place, Space and Gender* (Cambridge: Polity Press, 1994).

Massey, Doreen. 'Space-time and the Politics of Location', in Alan Read (ed.), *Architecturally Speaking* (London & New York: Routledge, 2000).

Massumi, Brian. 'Navigating Movements,' 2002 interview [online] http://www.brianmassumi.com/interviews/NAVIGATING%20MOVEMENTS.pdf.

Massumi, Brian. *Parables for the Virtual: Movement, Affect, Sensation* (Durham: Duke University Press, 2002).

Miller, Nancy K. *Getting Personal* (London & New York: Routledge, 1991).

Mock, Roberta. 'Introduction', in Roberta Mock (ed.), *Performing Processes: Creating Live Performance* (Bristol: Intellect, 2000).

Moorhouse, Paul. *Richard Long: Walking the Line* (London: Thames & Hudson, 2002).

Murray, Geoffrey. *The Gentle Art of Walking* (London: Blackie & Son, 1939).

      n, Shirley. 'Autobiography: From Different Poetics to a Poetics of Differences', in Marlene Kadar
           s on Life Writing: From Genre to Critical Practice (Toronto: University of Toronto Press,

Nielsen, Tom. 'The Return of the Excessive: Superfluous Places', *Space and Culture*, 5(1), 2002, pp. 53–62.

Pearson, Mike. 'Bubbling Tom', in Adrian Heathfield (ed.), *Small Acts: Performance, the Millennium and the Marking of Time* (London: Black Dog Publishing, 2000).

Pearson, Mike. *'In Comes I': Performance, Memory and Landscape* (Exeter: Exeter University Press, 2006).

Pearson, Mike and Michael Shanks. *Theatre/Archaeology: Disciplinary Dialogues* (London: Routledge, 2001).

Penrose, Roger. *The Large, the Small and the Human Mind* (Cambridge: Cambridge University Press, 2000).

Phelan, Peggy. *Mourning Sex* (London: Routledge, 1997).

Pile, Steve and Nigel Thrift. *Mapping the Subject: Geographies of Cultural Transformation* (London & New York: Routledge, 1995).

Probyn, Elspeth. 'Lesbians in Space. Gender, Sex and the Structure of Missing', *Gender, Place and Culture*, 2(1), 1995, pp. 77–84.

Probyn, Elspeth. 'Dis/connect: Space, Affect, Writing' [online] http://home.iprimus.com.au/painless/space/elspeth.html.

Rebellato, Dan. 'Playwriting and Globalization: Towards a Site-Unspecific Theatre', *Contemporary Theatre Review*, 16(1), 2006, pp. 97–113.

Reconstruction, 'Autobiogeography: Considering Space & Identity' issue, Summer 2002: 2(3) [online] http://reconstruction.eserver.org/023/TOC.htm.

Ross, Kristin. 'Lefebvre on the Situationists: An Interview with Kristin Ross', *October*, 79, 1997, pp. 68–83.

Roth, Moira (ed.) *Rachel Rosenthal* (Baltimore: The John Hopkins University Press, 1997).

Shoard, Marion. 'Edgelands', in Jennifer Jenkins (ed.), *Remaking the Landscape* (London: Profile Books, 2002).

Sinclair, Iain. *Edge of the Orison: In the Traces of John Clare's 'Journey Out of Essex'* (London: Hamish Hamilton, 2005).

Smith, Phil. 'Dread, Route and Time: An Autobiographical Walking of Everything Else', *Reconstruction*, 3(1), Winter 2003 [online] http://reconstruction.eserver.org/031/smith.htm.

Smith, Phil. 'A Short History of the Future of Walking', *Rhizomes* 7, Fall 2003 [online] http://www.rhizomes.net/issue7/smith.htm.

Smith, Phil. 'A Taxonomy on its Toes', *Performance Research*, 11(1), 2006, pp. 33–39.

Smith, Sidonie and Julia Watson (eds). *Getting a Life: Everyday Uses of Autobiography* (Minneapolis: University of Minnesota Press, 1996).

Smith, Sidonie and Julia Watson (eds). *Women, Autobiography, Theory: A Reader* (Madison: University of Wisconsin Press, 1998).

Smithson, Robert. *Robert Smithson: The Collected Writings*, Jack Flam (ed.) (Berkeley: University of California Press, 1996).

Solnit, Rebecca. *Wanderlust: A Short History of Walking* (London: Verso, 2001).

Soule, Lesley. *The Actor as Anti-Character: Dionysus, the Devil and the Boy Rosalind* (Westport: Greenwood Press, 2000).

Thomas, Sue. *Hello World: Travels in Virtuality* (York: Raw Nerve, 2004).

Turner, Cathy. 'Framing the Site', *Site-Specific: The Quay Thing Documented, Studies in Theatre and Performance*, Supplement 5, 2000.

Turner, Cathy. 'Palimpsest or Potential Space? Finding a Vocabulary for Site-Specific Performance', *New Theatre Quarterly*, 20(4), 2004, pp. 373–90.

Virilio, Paul. *Speed and War: An Essay on Dromology* (New York: Columbia University Press, 1986).

Wade, David. *Li: Dynamic Form in Nature* (New York: Walker & Co, 2003).

Walking in Place [online] http://www.walkinginplace.org/.

Wegener, Claudia. 'Manresa: Autobiography as Method ...', *Performance Research*, 7(3), 2002, pp. 30–46.

Williams, David. 'Frontwords', *Performance Resesarch: On Place*, 3(2), 1998, pp. v–viii.

Wilkie, Fiona. 'Mapping the Terrain: A Survey of Site-Specific Performance in Britain', *New Theatre Quarterly*, 70, 2002, pp. 140–60.

Wrights & Sites (Stephen Hodge, Simon Persighetti, Phil Smith, Cathy Turner). *An Exeter Mis-Guide* (Exeter: Wrights & Sites, 2003).

Wrights & Sites (Stephen Hodge, Simon Persighetti, Phil Smith, Cathy Turner). *A Mis-Guide to Anywhere* (Exeter: Wrights & Sites, 2006).

Wrights & Sites homepage [online] http://www.mis-guide.com/ws.html.

Biographical Notes

Deirdre (Dee) Heddon is a Reader in the Department of Theatre, Film and Television Studies at the University of Glasgow. She is the author of *Autobiography and Performance* (Palgrave Macmillan, 2008) and co-author of *Devising Performance: A Critical History* (Palgrave Macmillan, 2005) with Jane Milling. Dee's autobiographical performances include *Warden* (2001), *Forward to Sender* (2002), *Following in the Footsteps* (2002), and *One Square Foot Project (Tree)* (2003). Her most recent research focuses on the connections between forests and performance.

Carl Lavery is Senior Lecturer in Theatre at Aberystwyth University. He has published articles on various aspects of performance and is co-editor of *Jean Genet: Performance and Politics* (Palgrave Macmillan, 2006) and co-author of *Sacred Theatres* (2007). He has just finished working on an AHRC-funded project called 'Re-enchantment and Reclamation: New Perceptions of Morecambe Bay through Dance, Music and Sound'. Carl has recently completed a monograph *Spaces of Revolution: The Politics of Jean Genet's Late Theatre* for Manchester University Press. He is currently co-editing (with David Williams) a new volume on Lone Twin Theatre for Black Mountain Press and with (Clare Finburgh) a collection of essays on Contemporary French Theatre and Performance for Palgrave Macmillan.

Roberta Mock is Reader in Performance and Associate Dean for Research in the Faculty of Arts at the University of Plymouth. Her books include *Jewish Women on Stage, Film and Television* (Palgrave Macmillan, 2007) and, as editor: *Performing Processes: Creating Live Performance* (Intellect, 2000) and, with Colin Counsell, *Performance, Embodiment, and Cultural Memory* (Cambridge Scholars Publishing, forthcoming). She is currently co-writing a book entitled *Doing Performance Research* with Baz Kershaw and Gill Hadley for Palgrave Macmillan, and is developing solo performances and video work exploring cultural identity through re-enactment.

Phil Smith is a member of Wrights & Sites and one of the authors of *An Exeter Mis-Guide* (2003) and *A Mis-Guide To Anywhere* (2006). He has been the dramaturg for TNT (Munich) since 1981 and is the author of over 100 texts and libretti for theatres and music theatres including the St Petersburg State Comedy Theatre, Teatro Dionisio (Costa Rica) and Theater Am Sozialamt (Munich). His independent walking-based performances include *A Michael Chekhov Mis-Guide* (2006) with Simon Persighetti, *Mobile Machinoeki* (2007) with Anoushka Athique and Katie Etheridge, and *In Search of Pontiflunk* (2008) with New Perspectives Theatre Company. He is a Senior Research Associate at the University of Plymouth, and a Visiting Lecturer at the University of Exeter and at Dartington College of Arts.